Sketches of SAINTS Known & Unknown

J. P. Vaswani

Sterling Paperbacks

Books and Booklets By J.P. Vaswani

In English:

The Seven Commandments of the Bhagavad Gita
Kill Fear Before Fear Kills You
Swallow Irritation Before Irritation Swallows You
It's All A Matter of Attitude
You Can Make A Difference
101 Stories For You and Me
108 Pearls of Practical Wisdom
108 Simple Prayers of a Simple Man
108 Thoughts On Success
114 Thoughts on Love
A Child of God
A Day with Dadaji
A Mystic of Modern India
Begin the Day with God
Beloved Dadaji
Conversations with Dadaji
Dada Answers
Daily Appointment With God
Daily Inspiration
Doors of Heaven
Education: What India Needs
Feast of Love
Five Fragrant Flowers
From Darkness Into Light
From Hell to Heaven
Glimpses
Glimpses Into Great Lives
God In Quest of Man
Hinduism
How to Have Real Fun Out of Life and other Talks
How to Make Your Life A Love Story
How to Overcome Temptations
How to Overcome Tensions
I Have Need of You
I Luv U, God!
Invest in the Child
Joy Peace Pills
Laugh Your Way to Health
Life After Death
Life is A Love Story
Love and Laugh!
Nestle Now
Notes from the Master's Lute
Pictures and Parables
Positive Power of Thanksgiving
Prayers of a Pilgrim
Prophets and Patriots
Sadhu Vaswani: His Life and Teachings
Little Lamps
Secrets of Health and Happiness

Shanti Speaks
Snacks for the Soul
More Snacks for the Soul
Stories for Meditation
Stories for You and Me
Teach Me to Pray
Tear-Drops (poems)
Temple Flowers
Ten Commandents of A Successful Marriage
The Holy Man of Hyderabad
The Kingdom of Krishna
A Little Book of Life
A Little Book of Wisdom
The Little Book of Prayer
The Little Book of Service
The Little Book of Success
The Little Book of Yoga
The Little Book of Freedom From Stress
The Magic of Forgiveness
The Simple Way
The Story of A Simple Man
The Way of *Abhyasa* (How to Meditate)
Ticket to Heaven
Twinkle, Twinkle Tiny Star
What You Would Like to Know about *Karma*
Whispers
Why Do Good People Suffer?
You Are Not Alone!
You Can Be a Smile Millionaire
Destination Happiness
Ladder of *Abhyasa*
Peace or Perish – There is no Other Choice
Good Parenting
Teachers Are Sculptors
I am a Sindhi
The Perfect Relationship: Guru and Disciple

In Hindi:

Ishwar Tujhe Pranaam
Prarthna Ki Shakti
Alwar Santon Ki Mahaan Gaathaayein
Atmik Jalpaan
Atmik Poshan
Bhale Logon Ke Saath Bura Kyon
Chitra Darshan
Dainik Prerna
Krodh Ko Jalayen, Swayam Ko Nahi
Mahan Purush Jeevan Darshan
Santon Ki Lila
Mrityun Hai Dwaar Phir Kya
Safal Vivah Ka Dus Rahasya

Published by
Sterling Publishers Private Limited

STERLING PAPERBACKS
An imprint of
Sterling Publishers (P) Ltd.
A-59, Okhla Industrial Area, Phase-II,
New Delhi-110020.
Tel: 26387070, 26386209; Fax: 91-11-26383788
E-mail: sterlingpublishers@airtelmail.in
ghai@nde.vsnl.net.in
www.sterlingpublishers.com

Sketches of Saints: Known & Unknown
© 2008, J. P. Vaswani
ISBN 978 81 207 3998 7

All rights are reserved.
No part of this publication may be reproduced, stored in a retrieval system or transmitted, in any form or by any means, mechanical, photocopying, recording or otherwise, without prior written permission of the author.

Printed and Published by Sterling Publishers Pvt. Ltd.,
New Delhi-110 020.

Contents

Sant Kabir	1
Shankaracharya	25
Father Damien	42
Hasan *Darvesh*	53
Mother Teresa	64
Ishadassi	80
Albert Schweitzer	89
Sadhvi Vasuki	101
Sahl *Darvesh*	114
Sant Avvaiyar	121
Sadhu Hiranand	133
Sister Nivedita	142
Swami Rama Lingam	153

Sadhu Vaswani 165
Gurudev Ranade 193
Jose Rizal 202
Shabri 214
Swami Leela Shah 224
Sadna *Kasai* 231
Zarathustra 240

Sant Kabir

Kabir was truly a revolutionary among the ranks of India's great saints. Brought up as a devout Muslim, he boldly declared, "I am a child of Rama and Allah!" Impatient with ritualism, orthodoxy and the arid intellectualism of philosophy or metaphysics, his message was: "Children of God are ye all! Be One! Be united! Rise above rituals and ceremonies to the vision of Love." Is not this message the urgent need of India and the nations today? A saint who was centuries ahead of his time, Kabir expressed the most profound truths in the simplest images and words, which are held sacred by millions of people, even today.

Sant Kabir

India is considered to be the land of saints and sages. For centuries many saints have taken birth on the sacred soil of India and have influenced the lives of countless number of people. It can truly be said that no other country has been blessed with so many saints. One such saint, was Sant Kabir. In fact, he is regarded by many as a spiritual giant among saints. Some even regard him as a manifestation of God Himself.

Sant Kabir, appeared in the year 1398. Around that time, India was passing through a difficult period of her history. His arrival heralded a new era.

There are different accounts describing his birth. According to some of them we are told that, one day, a small child was found lying under a tree, sucking his thumb. His eyes shone brightly, and a beatific smile was on his face. Others say that a small child was found atop a lotus leaf in a lake in Banaras. Nobody really knows where and how he was born. Some are even of the opinion that pillars of light descended from Heaven, touched the waters of the lake, and thus, the child was created.

There is only one common ground of agreement that, during his childhood he was brought up in a poor Muslim family. The father's name was Niru, and the mother was Nima. Both Nima and Niru were illiterate and poor and belonged to the underprivileged class. They were childless, and having discovered the abandoned baby, took him home and brought him up as their own child.

A Kazi – Muslim priest – was called for the naming ceremony. When the Kazi opened the Holy Quran the first word spotted by him was Kabir. The Kazi closed his eyes, said his prayers and opened the Quran again. Again, his gaze fell on the word Kabir. Kabir is a Name of God. How could a child coming from this lowly background, be named after God? The meaning of the word Kabir is the Almighty One, the Highest One. The Kazi thought that it was inappropriate for this child to be given this name. So he asked them to wait awhile. Once again, he closed his eyes, offered a prayer and opened the Quran Sharif. His eyes fell on the word Akbar. Now Akbar is also another Name of God. *Allah-O-Akbar* – Allah, the greatest of the Great. The Kazi was bewildered. He felt that he could not, should not, give a child of a backward class, a name like Akbar.

In the meantime, Niru and Nima got impatient and did not want to wait anymore. They decided to name their child Kabir.

Both Niru and Nima loved Kabir dearly. Kabir's shining eyes and pleasant face attracted all. As he grew in age, he would often sit in a silent corner. His mother would call out to him, "My child Kabir, lend me a helping hand with the household work." His father would call him and say, "My son Kabir, I have woven the cloth, come, help me carry it to the marketplace to sell it." Kabir was always lost in his own thoughts.

As a child, Kabir's heart was full of mercy and compassion. On the occasion of *Bakri Id,* as per custom, an animal is bought and sacrificed ritually. The meat is cooked and distributed as holy *prasad*. Id was nearing, and Kabir's father said to him, "My child, we shall purchase a lamb and sacrifice it on the day of *Id*."

Kabir exclaimed, "Sacrifice it! What does that mean?"

The father explained, "According to our custom, we buy an animal, bring it home, feed it well and on the day of Id, sacrifice the animal. It is slaughtered and cut into pieces and cooked for the feast."

Hearing this, Kabir was horrified. He exclaimed, "Get it home? Feed it well and then slaughter and cut it into pieces? What kind of festivity is this?" It was beyond the child's understanding.

However, Niru brought the lamb and tied it up in the house. From that day, child Kabir was unable to eat a morsel. When food was brought to him, he refused to eat it, for he had lost his appetite. His parents asked him what was his problem? What had happened to him? Without answering, Kabir would go and sit near the lamb and shed tears. He would pat the lamb lovingly and would say, "Now you shall be with us only for a few days. After that, my father, with his own hands, will slaughter you."

The parents found it unbearable to see him crying. They said to him, "Son, you are the light of our eyes, the soul of our being. Why are you crying?"

Kabir said, "I am unable to take in the horror of what I have been told. I am unable to bear it. There is a storm of agony in my heart. This goat which we have kept with us and whom we have been feeding, we are going to slaughter it with our own hands! How can we do such a thing?"

Kabir was heartbroken. He could not partake of any food or drink. He spent sleepless nights. He would sit near the lamb and say, "God who has made me and my parents, the One who has made each and every creature, the same God has also made you. Then how can my father slaughter you? I am not able to understand this cruelty."

At last the father comprehends the great depth of sorrow and agony of his son. He promises him that he will not slaughter the lamb, nor will he sell it to anyone else. The lamb would stay with them as a member of their family. Hearing those words from the lips of his father, Kabir dances with joy. He literally jumps with delight. Was he not an angel of compassion?

Abstain from meat and fish. Treat all creatures with mercy and compassion. This was his teaching to all. He could not bear to see the pain and suffering of others.

One day, Kabir's father said to him, "Today, I am not feeling too well. I have woven the cloth, but will not be able to take it to the market-place."

His mother added, "There is not a grain of food in the house, that is why I would like you to go to the market-place and sell the cloth. You may be young, but you are intelligent and sensible. You are a child blessed with awareness and common sense. I believe, you will be able to sell the cloth, collect the money and buy food grains, so that we may have something to eat today."

Kabir was very pleased and thought to himself, "My father trusts me. I'll go to the market-place and sell the cloth and earn a lot of money and bring home the food grains. Then my parents will be proud of me." With these thoughts in his mind, Kabir was on his way to the market, when he came across an old, feeble person who was shivering with cold and crying out for help. "Is there anybody here to clothe me so that I can cover myself and keep myself warm?" he cried, "I cannot bear this terrible cold." Hearing this painful cry for help, Kabir thought, "I have a full load of cloth, this man requires just a little of it! I shall give him some cloth and sell the remaining at a good price and fulfill the requirements of the family. Father, on seeing the things I bring in exchange, will surely be satisfied. He will not even ask me whether I sold all the cloth or gave a part of it away."

Kabir cut some yards of cloth and spread it over the old and feeble-bodied man. He said to the old man, "Baba, you are like my father. I humbly offer this cloth to you, kindly accept it."

The old, feeble man looked at the attractive face of Kabir and said to him, "My child, there is so much love in your heart! No one has ever spoken to me the way you have done today. I salute you. May God's blessings be showered on you. But, I would like to tell you, back home I have a wife and children, and they too, are shivering in the cold. I'm not asking you for more cloth but I just thought that you should know. You are a small child, I do not want to deprive you further. I just want to convey this information to you."

Kabir's heart was so tender, kind and caring for others, that on hearing what the old man had to say, he forgot his errand and told him, "Take this whole load of cloth with you and protect your wife and children from the cold."

Kabir gave away all the cloth, but later it dawned on him, that he was supposed to bring back home flour, pulses, rice, etc. Where would he procure those from?

He roamed around in the streets for some hours, but being a small child, how long could he remain away from home? Finally, he did come back home. At home, his parents were waiting anxiously for his return. The father thought, "Why did I have to send such a small child to the market? Parhaps, on the way, someone might have grabbed the cloth from him and beaten him up. What have I done? What has become of my dear son?"

When they saw Kabir returning, their eyes shone in hope and happiness. They found his hands empty and felt that, perhaps, the food grains and other articles were being brought by someone who followed him. When Kabir told them of what had happened, they were deeply disappointed and angry with Kabir. But Kabir insisted, "Mamma, Papa, believe me, that poor man's need was much greater than our own!"

Gurudev Sadhu Vaswani said to us, "Never forget that the poor and needy, the forsaken and forlorn are pictures of God. To serve them is truly to worship God."

As Kabir grew in years, he kept asking himself, again and again, "What is the purpose for which I have been given this human birth? O Lord, grant me the strength and the wisdom to fulfill this purpose."

Kabir was in search of a Guru, who would guide him. When our thirsty hearts yearn for God, then the need for a Guru arises – a Guru who may hold our hand and lead us on – ever onward, forward, Godward!

Who is a Guru? A Guru is one who has not merely studied the Vedas and the Scriptures or one who reads a few books and gives discourses. A Guru is essentially a man of experience, of God-realisation. A true Guru is a friend of God. He walks with God. He talks to God. He lives and moves and has a perpetual fellowship with God. His every moment is spent in the presence of God. There is no difference, no separation, between such a person and God. To see such a one, is to see God Himself. Even if we were to go and meditate in the forest for several years, face hardships and practise austerities, or if we were to undertake a vow of silence or fast for years, or go on pilgrimages; it is nothing compared to spending a short time in the company of a true Guru!

To light a candle, you require another one that is already lit, or a matchstick. Similarly, to be able to kindle the light within, you require the company of a person who is already illumined. The Guru is an illumined soul; it is only he who can help enlighten another soul.

In the heart of Sant Kabir, was the deep longing to find a Guru. He saw people visiting temples and mosques, bathing in holy waters, fasting, performing rituals, and he thought: "I desire to go on a pilgrimage within, for which I need the guidance of a true Guru."

His quest took him to many a Muslim priest, but he saw that their lives were a facade. They read the Holy Quran, but there was no love for truth in their lives: they were prejudiced and differentiated between friends and enemies. They called the Hindus *kafirs*, infidels, and showed no mercy and kindness towards birds and animals. Like many common men, they lamented in sorrow and exulted in joy. They could not be true Gurus! He said to himself, "I need a Guru who will lead me to the Lotus Feet of God."

He prayed to Allah: "O Lord, You have not sent me to this earth-plane to waste my life in vain, by frittering it away in pursuit of pleasures. You have given me this human birth to become one with You. Bring me into contact with a realised soul who can lead me to You."

In those days there was a great saint named Ramanand. Kabir wanted to make Ramanand his Guru, but Ramanand, in the interest of peace among communities, was not prepared to accept a Muslim as his disciple. However, Kabir was determined to have Ramanand as his Guru. He learnt that Ramanand began his day by taking a dip in the sacred Ganges at four in the morning, after which he would sit for his daily prayers.

One day, Kabir awoke before four in the morning and lay down on one of the steps that led to the river bank. Sant Ramanand, as was his daily routine, proceeded to the river in the dark of the dawn, chanting the Name of Rama. As he went down the steps that led to the river, suddenly his feet touched the body of a man lying on the steps. He exclaimed loudly, 'Rama, Rama, Rama'.

On hearing the words, 'Rama, Rama, Rama', Kabir immediately got up and clapped his hands in the joy of having found a Guru and received the *Guru mantra*. "I have received what I intensely longed for," he exclaimed.

From that day onwards, Kabir started telling everyone, "Sant Ramanand is my Guru and, in his mercy, he has given me a *Guru-mantra*."

When Ramanand learnt of this, he sent for Kabir and said to him, "I have never accepted you as my disciple. Nor do I remember having given you a *mantra!*"

Kabir reminded him of the incident that had happened a few days earlier, saying, "Gurudev, when you trampled over my body, I held your feet in my hands and you uttered Rama, Rama, Rama, which I took as my *Guru-mantra*."

Sant Ramanand did remember the incident and became speechless. He could not contradict Kabir. He smiled and said to Kabir, "My child, you win – and I lose!"

Kabir was happy, he had found a true Guru. And he boldly declared that he was a child of both Rama and Allah. He propagated the truth that God is One, though He is called by many Names.

Kabir always thought of God as the Formless One and did not believe in idol worship. He said, "The Lord is seated in everyone's heart. Everyone can speak to Him and can hear Him speak. God does not dwell on a distant star. He is wherever we are. He is here, He is now. God can be felt, He can be touched. And, instead of going to temples and so-called holy places, one should enter on the interior pilgrimage."

One day, as was the custom, Ramanand had a *puja* performed for his ancestors. The *puja* included feeding crows and animals. Rice and other foods were cooked specially for the purpose. Ramanand asked that the food should be spread on the ground for the birds to come and eat it, so that it would reach the ancestors. At this, Kabir remarked that the food would be eaten by the crows, and would not reach the ancestors at all. It dawned on Ramanand, that what Kabir said was, indeed, the truth. After this incident, Ramanand became more liberal in his thinking and realised that many customs were no better than superstitions.

In the days of Sant Kabir, people would go to the forest to meditate, and because of this they would be regarded as saintly souls. Sant Kabir explained to the people, that instead of going to the forest, one needed to go deep within oneself.

Be in the world, but be not worldly, taught Kabir. Therefore, grow in the inner spirit of detachment. Do your duties, fulfil your obligations, but all the time let the thought of God be in the background of your consciousness. The disease from which most of us suffer is the disease of forgetfulness. The mind always keeps on wandering and we keep on wandering with the mind.

This wandering is the root cause of our unhappiness. If only our minds are fixed on God, all our unhappiness would vanish as mist before the morning sun.

According to Sant Kabir, those living in their families could attain God more easily than those who renounced the family-life. Kabir himself had a family of his own. His wife was Loi: she, too, was a devotee of the Lord. They had two children, a son named Kamaal and a daughter called Kamaali. The four of them lived in a small cottage.

According to Kabir's teachings, the first principle of righteous living is to revere the guest, to welcome and serve him as though he were an Image of God. A guest is called an *"atithi"* which means one, who announces himself without previous intimation. This, said Kabir, is a quality of God: and the guest must be treated as God.

Sant Kabir himself bore witness to this ideal and lovingly served guests and *sadhus* who came to his hut without previous intimation. His hut was a small one and could contain only four beds. Almost everyday there were some guests to be looked after. And the four beds were occupied by the guests. The members of the family would gladly sleep on the floor. The food would first be served to the guests and what was left over would be eaten by the family members. Yet, all the four regarded themselves as among the happiest of humans.

We are told that, one evening, when it was raining very heavily, a few *sadhus* arrived at the cottage of Sant Kabir and said to him, "We have heard a lot about you and your spirit of hospitality. We seek to be your guests for a few hours, and share a meal with you."

Sant Kabir welcomed them with open arms and a warm heart. He asked his wife, Loi, what food she could serve to the guests. Loi replied that right then, there was *nothing* in the house which could be offered to the guests: all the groceries had been consumed.

Kabir told his wife that he had woven some cloth which could be sold. But, unfortunately, the *bazar* was closed and besides, it was raining heavily. When the rain stopped, he would go and sell the cloth. In the meantime, he asked her if there was any shop nearby from where they could receive groceries on credit.

In answer Loi said to her husband, "Beloved, you know very well that there is no shop which would give us food on credit. As we are poor, they always ask for money first, and only then give us groceries."

Kabir was unperturbed. He said, "God who has sent those guests will Himself provide food for them."

He asked his wife to go to the market and find if some shopkeeper would give her the required groceries. In obedience, Loi went from one shop to another, asking for credit. But no shopkeeper was prepared to oblige. At last, she reached one shop whose owner was a young man. Loi was a pretty woman. The young man looked at her and said that he would oblige on one condition: that she would spend the night with him.

Loi was appalled to hear this. How could any man utter such words to a married woman? Loi always had a sweet smile on her face and the shopkeeper misunderstood the smile. Thinking that she had agreed to his condition, he told her to take whatever she needed. Loi brought the commodities home and served the guests who felt exceedingly happy to get such a feast.

After dinner the guests left: it was then that Loi narrated the story of the young shopkeeper to her husband. Sant Kabir said to his wife, "It is getting dark and the young man must be waiting for you. I shall take you there, but since it is pouring outside, cover yourself with a blanket."

Sant Kabir carried his wife, Loi, on his shoulders and arrived at the house of the shopkeeper. He waited outside the house while Loi went in. The shop-owner was astonished to see her. In spite of the heavy downpour, he found that her clothes were dry and her feet were clean. He questioned Loi who replied that her husband had brought her on his own shoulders. Hearing this, the shop owner was taken aback. How could a husband bring his own wife in the dark of the night to the house of a man whose intentions were impure!

The shopkeeper realised that the husband was no ordinary man, and he felt extremely guilty. He felt ashamed of his conduct. He wanted to know more about her husband.

Loi said to the young man, "Sant Kabir is the name of my husband and he is waiting outside."

The shop owner, with tears in his eyes, asked Loi to be forgiven for his misconduct. He requested her to take him to her husband. He fell at the feet of Sant Kabir and begged for forgiveness. Kabir embraced him and told him that he had been forgiven and that he must forget all that had happened. From then on, the shopkeeper became a faithful disciple of Sant Kabir and said to him, "Henceforth, I and my shop and all it contains belong to you!"

Sant Kabir was a rare and unique saint. He often said, This earth is not our home. It is a travellers' inn; our stay here is for a brief while. He also said, This earth is a school where we have come to learn lessons we need to learn. But coming here, we have forgotten the purpose of our visit and easily yield to temptations of lust, hatred, greed, egoism.

He taught that each one of us is in reality a swan bird, pure, white, radiant – but coming here, we have drunk the wine of *maya* and, in the intoxication of pelf, pleasure and power, we have forgotten our true selves. Thus, the swan thinks of himself as a crow.

Kabir's clarion-call to everyone who met him or joined his fellowship was: "O swan-bird of the Soul, speak to me of your true Homeland, where you really belong. You are not a creature of the earth, earthy. You are an immortal Soul!"

In a number of *slokas* and songs, Sant Kabir speaks of the perfect relationship – the relationship between the Guru and the disciple. It is a tender, unique and pure relationship. All other relationships come to an end one day or the other. At most they last as long as the body lasts. But the relationship between the Guru and the disciple is eternal. It endures, birth after birth.

The Guru is the true friend of the disciple. The Guru always dwells in the mind of the disciple. In every birth the Guru himself finds his disciple; it is not necessary that the disciple has to go out in search of the Guru. All that is required is deep yearning, intense longing of the heart for the Guru.

Sant Kabir never regarded himself as a Guru. He said, I am a servant of all! Yet, there were many who thought of themselves as disciples of Sant Kabir.

One of them was Dharamdas. He was a rich businessman who strongly believed in idol worship. One day, before he met Sant Kabir, he sat on the banks of the river Ganges, worshipping, as was his wont, his idols. Sant Kabir happened to pass by. He looked at Dharamdas: he recognised his disciple, though the disciple did not recognise the Guru!

Sant Kabir sat by the side of Dharamdas and greeted him with a smile. Then, pointing to one of the idols, Sant Kabir said, that it could well be used as a weight on the weighing scales, in Dharamdas' shop!

Dharamdas naturally was annoyed. He felt that his Gods were being insulted by the strange intruder. He stared angrily at Sant Kabir.

Sant Kabir said to him, "My friend, do not be angry. But tell me, have the idols ever conversed with you? You have prayed to them for years; do you get any reply from them in return? Have they ever spoken to you? Have they ever responded to any of your prayers?"

Dharamdas continued to stare at Sant Kabir with angry eyes: and Sant Kabir quickly left the place.

Dharamdas could not forget Kabir and his words. They kept ringing in his ears. When, after some time, Dharamdas cooled down, he began to reflect on the words of Sant Kabir. He realised that what Sant Kabir had told him was absolutely right. He had worshipped idols for a long time, but they had never spoken to him or responded to his prayers.

A few months later, while Dharamdas was performing a *puja* in which the *havan* fire was to be kept burning, Sant Kabir passed by. Both looked at each other. Dharamdas did not recognise Sant Kabir, who said to him, "You are a sinner! What are you doing?"

By the side of Dharamdas was his wife, Amnadevi. When she heard the strong words uttered by Kabir, she flared up and said: "My husband is a great devotee of God. How dare you call him a sinner? It is *you* who are a sinner!"

Sant Kabir looked at Amnadevi and Dharamdas with compassionate eyes, and said to them, "The wood and sticks which you are offering in the holy fire, are infected with insects which are being burnt alive."

Dharamdas examined a stick and found small insects crawling on it.

Dharamdas and his wife realised their mistake. But, in the meantime, Kabir was gone! Dharamdas looked for him but could not find him. He said to his wife, "I think this man was the same one who, months ago, had spoken objectionable words about the idols. I wanted to meet him and request him to accept me as his disciple. But you spoke so rudely to him – and he is gone! How shall I find him again?"

His wife said to him, "That is very simple. Let us perform a big *yagna* and announce that all saints and holy men are invited to participate. We will give them a lot of *dakshina*. Where there is honey, flies will automatically come and congregate. And you will easily find the one whom you seek."

Elaborate arrangements for a magnificent *yagna* were made. It was publicised, far and wide. Saints from different parts of the country participated in the sacrificial ceremony. But the one for whom Dharamdas eagerly waited did not arrive. The *yagna* concluded, but Sant Kabir did not come.

Dharamdas performed many more *yagnas* in different towns and villages, but Kabir didn't make his appearance. Dharamdas kept spending all the wealth he had, to find the Saint who had captured his heart, but whose name he did not know. Until finally, he spent all he had over a *yagna* which was held at Mathura, on the banks of the Yamuna river.

Now he became dejected and depressed. He had no money left. He said to himself, "I have spent all my wealth but have not achieved the goal. Let me not live any longer. Let me end my life by jumping into the Yamuna River."

There he stood on the banks of the Yamuna, ready to jump into the vast expanse of the waters, when he felt someone pulling him from behind. He turned back and there he saw the Beloved of his heart, Sant Kabir.

"Where were you all this time?" he asked Sant Kabir, falling at his feet. "I wanted to offer you all my wealth but did not find you. Now that I have spent my all and have nothing to offer you, you have come to me."

Sant Kabir picked up Dharamdas and embraced him and said to him, "I was waiting for this moment when you have nothing to give or else you would have felt that I, too, was one of the flies that congregate where there is honey."

The relationship between the Guru and the disciple – between Kabir and Dharamdas – grew in strength as time passed. Until Dharamdas completely lost himself in the Guru and exclaimed, "I am not: alone the Guru abides!"

Gradually, the influence of Kabir grew from more to more. Kabir's discourses attracted many seekers. Everyday, more and more people gathered to listen to him.

Kabir sang many a song. His language and style were simple and direct. Though centuries have passed, Kabir's songs and *slokas* continue to be sung in numerous homes and temples, with fervour and devotion.

Sant Kabir continued to live in Kashi. On the opposite bank of the sacred river Ganges was a small town called Maghar. It was believed that whoso breathed his last in Kashi would reach the gates of Heaven, and whoso passed away in Maghar, would go to Hell. To educate the people, Kabir asked his followers to take him to Maghar, where he breathed his last.

When Kabir died, his body was claimed by both Hindus and Muslims. The Hindu followers wished to cremate the body, the Muslim followers wished to bury it. There is a story which tells us that while the Hindus and Muslims were engaged in a dispute, a little child lifted the shroud – and found that the body was gone! Instead there was a heap of flowers.

Truly, Kabir lived like a flower. Wherever he went, he spread the fragrance of his love-filled life. His teaching can be summed up in two words: Detach – Attach. Detach yourself from the world – its pelf, pleasure, power: and attach yourself to the Lotus Feet of the Lord – where alone is love, joy and peace. Let us live in the world – but let us not allow the world to live within us. Or, as Sri Ramakrishna often said, "Let the boat float over the waters but, let not water enter the boat."

Sayings of Sant Kabir

"I wandered far and wide!
I found Him not!
I gazed into my Heart
There, there, I beheld
The Beauteous One!"

* * * * *

"O servant! where dost thou seek Me?
Lo! I am beside thee.
Neither in temple nor in mosque am I.
Not in *Ka'aba*, nor in *Kailas* am I, thy Lord!
Not in rites nor in ceremonies.
If thou be a true seeker, thou shalt
See Me and meet Me in a single moment!
For God, saith Kabir, is the Breath of all breaths!"

* * * * *

"Go where you will,
To Kashi or to Mathura,
What do you gain if you do not see
The Vision within you?"

* * * * *

"O Swan of the soul! O bird of my heart!
Tell me thy ancient tale!
Tell me where is thy Homeland?
Tell me, too, what seekest thou here?
Awake! my Swan, awake! This very morn awake!
Arise! and follow me! And I shall take thee
To a Land where doubt nor sorrow rules:
Where the sting of death hath ceased!
I shall take thee to a Land
Where trees and woods of spring in beauty bloom,
And the bee of the heart,
Immersed in the nectar of the Name,
Desireth no other joy!
Awake! Arise! And follow me!"

Some Books by Sant Kabir

- Part of the Guru Granth Sahib: *Bhagat Bani* – 227 *Padas* in 17 *ragas* and 237 *slokas*.
- *One Hundred Poems of Kabir* – Translated by Rabindranath Tagore
- *Kabir: The Weaver's Songs* – Translated by Vinay Dharwadker
- *Kabir: Ecstatic Poems* – Translated by Robert Bly
- *Songs of Kabir* – Translated by Evelyn Underhill and Rabindranath Tagore
- *The Bijak of Kabir* – Translated by Linda Hess and Shukdev Singh
- *Ocean of Love*: The Anurag Sagar of Kabir
- *Songs of Kabir from the Adi Granth* – by Nirmal Dass

Some Books on Sant Kabir

- *Kabir: Biography and Philosophy* – by Ram Kumar Varma
- *Kabir* – by Mohan Singh Karki
- *Bharat Ke Sant Kavi Mahatma Kabir* – by Dr. Giriraj Sharan Agarwal
- *Kabir and The Kabir Panth* – by C H Westcott
- *A New Look At Kabir* – by Krishna P. Bahadur
- *Kabir the Great Mystic* – by Isaac A. Ezekiel
- *Lord Kabir* – by Sharan Malhotra
- *Kabir - The Weaver of God's Name* – by V. K. Sethi

Shankaracharya

India pays homage not to kings and emperors who fought and won great victories, but to sages and saints who have led a life of self-denial and service to suffering humanity. One of the greatest amongst them was **Sri Shankaracharya**. He was at once a saint and a scholar, a spiritual leader and an intellectual giant. He was a mighty force in the restitution of the *Sanatana Dharma* which is eternal and can never die! He was a great teacher who taught that the phenomenal universe was not a manifestation but a creation. The Creator is not separate from the creation. The One has become many.

Shankaracharya

From times immortal, India has produced a number of great teachers, great preceptors of *gnana* and *bhakti* – wisdom and devotion. One of the greatest among them was Sri Shankaracharya.

We owe a debt of gratitude to this great Acharya of India. Had it not been for the contribution of Sri Shankaracharya, *Bharatvarsha** would have ceased to be *Bharatvarsha* several centuries ago, and would never have survived the effects of mass conversions which were rampant in those days.

What were those days like? Chaos prevailed in the spheres of religion and philosophy. Sect after sect sprang up, and each claimed its superiority. Men were caught up in a snare of rites and rituals. Confusion, superstition and bigotry reigned supreme and the once glorious land of the Aryans was in a pitiable state.

During those turbulent times, Shri Adi Shankara was born in the small village of Kaladi, in Kerala, in the eighth century A.D. His father's name was Siva

---

* India

Guru and his mother was named Aryamba. Although they had been married for several years, they were childless. They were advised to go to a temple of Shiva, where they prayed continuously for three years. Their prayers were answered and a son was born to them; their happiness knew no bounds! They said, "This child is truly a gift from Lord Shiva." They named the child, Shankara. The father had this strong belief that it was Lord Shiva who had himself taken the form of a human being and blessed their home.

The child was very different from other children! He was endowed with wonderful intelligence. He had a prodigious memory. If he heard anything just once, he would remember it all his life. His mother took special care to educate her son in the study of various scriptures. When Shankara was five years old, he was sent to the *Gurukul*. At the *Gurukul,* students were expected to go and beg for their food, as was the ordained practice of *bal brahmacharis* or young ascetics.

One day, child Shankara went out to beg. He knocked at the door of a house and said: "Mother, please give me alms." He received no reply. He repeated his request. A lady came out and, seeing the little boy begging, sadly exclaimed, "There is nothing in the house to offer you, my child!"

Shankara understood the situation. "Mother," he said innocently, "I shall be content with whatever you give me and I shall pray that henceforth there will be no scarcity in your home."

The lady was perplexed. "What should I offer to this child?" she asked herself. She recalled that gooseberries grew in her backyard. She plucked them and offered them to Shankara. Shankara accepted them with gratitude and offered a prayer to Lakshmi, the Goddess of Wealth, to shower her benedictions on the woman. To her utter amazement, when the woman returned inside the house, she saw a shower of golden gooseberries in her backyard!

Within three years, Shankara had memorised the Vedas, the Upanishads and a number of other scriptures. His teachers said to him: "Now, you can return to your home. We have nothing further to teach you. You have become so knowledgeable that you can teach us."

Once when Shankara's father had to travel to a different town, he said to his son, "Shankara, everyday I worship God and offer *naivedya*. In my absence do likewise."

Shankara promised to do as he was told. The next day, he poured some milk in a cup and offered it to the idol with a prayer, "Lord, do kindly accept this offering." He waited for long. The deity did not accept the milk. The cup remained full. Shankara was disappointed.

With tear-filled eyes he prayed again, "Everyday you accept the offering of my father. What sin have I committed that you refuse to accept my offering?" He prayed earnestly: he prayed with tears in his eyes: but the offering remained untouched.

Finally, the little child said, "I promised my father that I would worship you even as he does, but you, O Lord, refuse to accept the offering. What shall I do? Let me kill myself." He ran out and brought a stone to kill himself. He was about to strike when, suddenly, the deity manifested itself and drank the entire cup of milk. Shankara was filled with joy.

When he was very young, Shankara lost his father. His mother continued to take great care of him. The mother was extremely attached to her son. As Shankara studied and meditated on the teaching of the scriptures, within his heart grew a feeling of *vairagya*, detachment. The longing within him grew to renounce the world and become a *sanyasi*. He said to himself: "This human birth is a golden opportunity which has been given to me, so that I may realise the Truth, which for want of a better word, men call God or *Brahman*."

Shankara spoke to his mother, seeking her permission to renounce the world, but she would not hear of it. She said to Shankara: "Your father has passed away. You are my only hope, my support and stay. You are the light of my life. If you leave me, I will not be able to live any longer. You must never think of renouncing the world."

As Shankara entered deeper and deeper into the silences of the soul that are within each one of us, he heard Voices. He spoke of it to his mother. "Ma," he would say to her, "voices are calling me! They are telling me: 'Come to us and we shall reveal to you the mystery of life and death.' Ma, will you not let me go?" The mother would not hear of it. On the contrary, she felt that if she got her son married, his mind-set might change. She spoke of this to Shankara. He begged his mother never to speak to him of marriage. "What have I to do with marriage?" he said. "Marriage is *maya* – bondage. I long for a life of freedom and fulfillment!"

One day, Shankara and his mother went to take a bath in the river. Shankara was a good swimmer. While swimming, Shankara strayed a bit too far. Suddenly, the mother heard a loud scream, "Ma! Ma! I am going!"

The mother asked, "My child, where are you going? How can I live without you?"

"Ma, a crocodile has caught me by the heel of my foot," Shankara cried out. "Now, any moment, he will swallow me up."

What could the poor mother do? She cried for help. The people said to her, "No one can save your son from the clutches of the crocodile!"

Shankara called out to the mother: "Ma! Anyway I am dying! Even now, if you give me permission to become a *sanyasi*, I can adopt *apad-sanyas* and have the satisfaction of dying as a *sanyasi*."

The mother said to herself, "What my son says is true. The crocodile will not let go of him. Let me give him the permission he asks for. Let him have the joy of dying as a *sanyasi!*"

She called out to her son, "My child, gladly do I permit you to enter *sanyasa*."

Quickly, Shankara took the vow of *sanyasa*. And a miracle happened! The crocodile let go of his foot. Shankara was able to emerge from the river alive and happy – blood dripping out of his heel.

At first, the mother was unable to believe what she saw. Was it just a trick Shankara had played on her? But the heel was bleeding profusely, and it carried the marks of the crocodile's teeth.

Shankara said to his mother, "Ma, you very kindly permitted me to enter *sanyasa* and God, in His mercy, has given me a new lease of life. Now I must go to attend to the work that awaits me."

"My child," said the mother, "I can't understand all that is happening. This is nothing short of a miracle. Surely, there is God's Hand in it. By all means, go and attend to the work for which God has sent you. But give me a promise that you will be with me during the last moments of my earth-pilgrimage. In this wide, vast world, I am all alone."

Shankara gave the promise to his mother and set out in quest of a Guru. "I have studied the *Shastras*, I have memorised the Vedas and the Upanishads," he said to himself. "But I need a Guru who can guide me on the Path, one who will remove the veils of ignorance and help me to see the Light."

Lost in those thoughts, Shankara continued to walk on, till he reached the banks of the river Narmada.

There he came to know of the great Guru, Govind Gaurapad. Shankara came to him and, bowing low at his feet, said to him, "Master! would you be so gracious as to accept me as your disciple? I wish to serve you. You are an enlightened soul. You walk with God: You talk to Him. Will you very kindly hold me by the hand and take me on the Path that leadeth to God? I surrender myself to You!"

Govind Gaurapad looked at Shankara, then closed his eyes. After sometime he opened them and said, "My child! Though you are young in years, you have the intellectual and spiritual attributes of a true devotee of God. I will initiate you and you will stay with me for some time. Then you will have to go and do the work for which God has sent you to this earth-plane."

Shankara stayed with his Guru for some time and served him as only a disciple can serve his master. The *ashram* of the Guru was situated on the banks of the Narmada. A time came when the river Narmada was in spate. The waters kept on rising. The cave where the Guru, Govind Gaurapad, lived was in danger of being flooded. Shankara was worried. He said, "My Gurudev's *kutiya* will get submerged in the rising waters!"

He went and stood, facing the angry waters of the river, and dipping his feet into the rising waters, recited the *Jalakarshan Mantra*, to pacify the waters of the river. He kept his *karmandal* (begging bowl) on the ground and began to pray. And a miracle was enacted! As soon as his feet touched the waters, the level of the river started receding. The people heaved a sigh of relief. All was safe!

When Shankara's Guru, Govind Gaurapad, witnessed this miracle, he observed, "Although Shankara is only nine or ten years of age, he is not an ordinary mortal. He is one blessed with special powers." The Guru was reminded of a prophecy made to him, years ago, by Maharishi Aatri. The sage had said to him, "There will come to the banks of the Narmada, one who can stop a flood with the power of his *mantra*. It will be he, who is the one person qualified and fit to write a commentary on the *Brahma Sutras*."

The Guru now directed Shankara to proceed to Kashi to study further and to cogitate on the teachings received from him. "Go and attend to the task that awaits you," he said to his disciple, "The great task of writing appropriate commentaries on the *Brahma Sutras*, the *Srimad Bhagavad Gita* and the *Upanishads*."

In Kashi, Shankara began to give discourses. People heard him – and were lost in wonder. Many came from distant places to listen to this young prodigy. He gave discourses on the *Gita*, the *Brahma Sutras* and the *Upanishads*. Learned people, distinguished teachers and priests listened attentively to the words of wisdom that fell from his lips – words more precious than pearls. They exclaimed, "Though he is young in years, the words that drop out of his lips are touched with a profound meaning." There were also some who did not accept what he said: they criticised his teaching. Quietly and convincingly, he answered the criticisms leveled against him.

Many earnest young aspirants were drawn to Shankaracharya. The first among them was Vishnu Sharma. Shankaracharya gave him a new name, Sunandan. Many more disciples followed Sunandan, to learn at the feet of Sri Shankara.

One day, Shankaracharya went to the river to bathe. After bathing, he strolled on the bank of the river. Some of his disciples were with him. He told them, "Come, today, we will all go to the temple of Vishwanath." As we know, in Kashi there is a magnificent Vishwanath temple. Pilgrims, in thousands, visit this temple everyday and offer obeisance to Lord Shiva.

Sri Shankara and his disciples set out for the Vishwanath temple. As they walked along the road, a person belonging to a low caste crossed their path. There was a bowl in his hand containing what looked like alcohol. There was also a dog following him. Seeing this *chandala*, the disciples signalled him to step aside. The man smiled and said, "Mahatma, you are asking me to move away. But first tell me, how I should move away? Should I move my body or my soul? Everyone's body is made of the same five elements. The makeup of my body is the same as yours. And the *Atman*, the soul, is one. So who has to move away from whom?"

Shankara was struck by the man's wisdom. He realised that it was no ordinary *chandala* who had crossed his path. This was none other than Lord Shiva who had come to teach him a lesson. He prostrated at the feet of the *chandala*. And he sang: "I see Thy image in all – alike in the Guru, as in the so-called low-caste person!" How true it is, that we all are one – children of the One Divine Father, God.

A few days later, Shankaracharya encountered a young student, who was trying to memorise a passage from a book. Sri Shankara admonished him, "My friend, this knowledge which you are trying to obtain from books is useless. True knowledge is of the heart." Again, he burst forth into song:

> "O friend, give your love to Govinda:
> With silent, swift foot-steps,
> Death cometh to overtake us,
> And take us to yonder Shore!
> Of what use is this false knowledge?
> Fill your heart with the love of God:
> Nothing else counts!"

Shankaracharya continued to stay in Kashi for a few years. Then, he set out on his travels, visiting town after town, village after village, enlightening the people with his wisdom. His presence was a benediction. He transformed the lives of many.

Once, while visiting Mahishmati he met Mandana Misra – the Chief Pandit of Mahishmati. Misra was a great scholar, who had developed a deep hatred for *sanyasis*. As soon as he saw Shankara, he lost his temper. Shankara challenged him to a debate: it was agreed that if Shankara lost, he would give up *sanyasa* and become a householder. And, if Misra was defeated, he would receive *sanyasa*. Bharati, the wife of Misra, was to be the judge.

Such debates were in the philosophical traditions of our country in those days. The one who lost a debate would become the disciple of the winner, acknowledging his intellectual and spiritual superiority.

A fierce debate ensued. It continued for days without a break. Bharati could not be present throughout. She placed a garland over the shoulders of both the debators and said, "He whose garland begins to fade first, should consider himself defeated." The debate lasted for seventeen long days, when the garland of Misra began to fade, and he accepted defeat.

However, Bharati interrupted, with a view to save her husband. She said, "The wife is the better half of her husband. You have vanquished only one half in the debate, now you have to vanquish me, too." Shankara objected to this interruption, but Bharati would not give up. Finally, Shankara relented. For a few more days the debate continued. The discussion led from one scripture to another. Finally, Bharati realised that on the plane of spiritual knowledge she could never, ever hope to vanquish Shankara. She decided to defeat him by posing questions on the *grahstha* (married) aspect of life, and asked him questions on the *Kama Shastra* – the art of love. What would a *sanyasi* know about this aspect of life? Shankara realised that, as he had no experience of *grahstha*, he would be no match for Bharati. He asked for a month's break before the discussion could continue. Bharati agreed.

Shankara returned to Kashi. There, he moved out of his physical body and, through transmigration, entered the body of a King, named Amaruka, who had just died. He asked his disciples to guard his own physical body into which, he said, he would re-enter after acquiring the knowledge he sought.

Suddenly, the dead body of the king stirred and he became alive. The ministers and the king's men were amazed to see the king open his eyes. The king got up as though out of a sleep. There was rejoicing all around.

Shankara gained the required experiences after living with the queens. He then returned to his body, entered it, and proceeded to Mahishmati to continue the debate with Bharati. This time, he was able to vanquish her. Misra became a disciple of Shankara and was initiated by him.

Shankaracharya then set out on a *pada yatra* (travelling on foot). While travelling, suddenly he felt that his mother wanted him. He immediately returned to his village, Kaladi. He saw that his mother was quite ill and felt that she would soon pass away. He said to her, "Mother, you are not this body. You are the

Atman. And the *Atman* cannot die or be destroyed. Fires cannot burn it, waters cannot drown it and winds cannot dry it." This is one of those rare instances, when a son becomes his mother's Guru and passes on *Atmavidya* to her. Having received this immortal teaching, the mother passed away, peacefully. Shankaracharya, with his own hands, performed the funeral rites and once again proceeded on his *yatra*.

He established four *Maths* or centers, at Dwarka, Badrinath, Shringeri and Jagannath Puri. Even today, these Maths carry on the great work of their founder.

Among the most prominent disciples of Shankara are four — Padmapada, Sureshwara, Hastamalaka and Trotaka. Shankara nominated them as the chiefs of the four *Maths*.

It is said, that Sri Shankara then travelled to Kedarnath, for he knew that his earthly life was drawing to a close. One morning, his disciples saw him enter a Himalayan cave — never to return.

Let us prostrate at the feet of this great mastermind and giant soul of India. A spiritual philosopher, Sri Shankaracharya was an impressive blend of knowledge and wisdom, faith and devotion. His scholarly erudition and masterly exposition of intricate philosophy have won him admiration throughout the world. Let us pay our homage to him.

Sayings of Shankaracharya

"I am neither ears nor tongue,
Nor senses of smell and sight,
Nor hands, nor feet:
Nor am I ether, fire, water, air!
I am pure Knowledge: I am unbroken Bliss!
I am Shiva! I am Shiva!
I have no form or fancy:
All-pervading am I – the *Atman:*
And beyond the senses am I!
Pure Knowledge and Bliss am I!
I am Shiva! I am Shiva!"

* * * * *

"There are three things which are rare indeed and are only due to the grace of God – namely, a human birth, the longing for Liberation, and the protecting care of a perfected sage."

* * * * *

"He who is free from the terrible snare of the hankering after sense-objects, so very difficult to get rid of, is alone fit for Liberation, and none else – even though he be versed in all the six *Shastras*."

* * * * *

"Just as a lamp illumines a jar or a pot, so also the *Atman* illumines the mind and the sense organs, etc. These material-objects by themselves cannot illumine themselves because they are inert."

* * * * *

"While practising *Samadhi* there appear unavoidably many obstacles, such as lack of inquiry, idleness, desire for sense-pleasure, sleep, dullness, distraction, tasting of joy, and the sense of blankness. One desiring the knowledge of Brahman should slowly get rid of such innumerable obstacles."

Some Works of Shankaracharya

- *Vivekachudamani*
- *Upadesa Sahasri*
- *Aparokshanubhuti*
- *Atma Bodha*
- *Vakya Sudha*
- *Tattva Bodha*
- *Vakya Vritti*
- *Panchikaranam*
- *Shivananda Lahari*
- *Soundarya Lahari*
- *Nirguna Manasa Puja*
- *Kanakadhara Stotram*
- *Bhaja Govindam*

Some Books on Shankaracharya

- *Acharya Shankara* – by Apurvananda
- *Vivekachudamani: The Crest Jewel of Wisdom, Attributed to Shankaracharya*
- *Lives of Saints* – by Swami Sivananda
- *Spiritual Import of Religious Festivals* – by Sri Swami Krishnananda
- *Shankara* – by Swami Sivananda
- The Advaita Philosophy of Sri Shankara – From Swami Sivananda's book '*All About Hinduism*'

Father Damien

Father Damien was one of the greatest heroes of humanity, a saint whose life shines in the beauty of love and sacrifice. He did not make any significant intellectual or theological contribution to Christianity. His contribution was his own life of noble deeds, a life of selfless service of lepers who, in his days, were regarded as loathsome untouchables. He built homes and churches for them. He opened schools for their children. He encouraged them to work and play – until he became a leper himself, and died for the love of his Master.

Father Damien

*S*ant Kabir sings in one of his *slokas:*
"I have dedicated my body and soul to Him. May I lay down my life for Him, and not forget Him in the hour of death!"

As I recite these memorable lines, my thoughts move out to one who, indeed, laid down his life for the Lord – Father Damien. He has been rightly called the Saint of Honolulu and Hawaii.

Born on January 3, 1840, in Belgium, he was the seventh of eight children. He was baptized as Joseph. As a boy, he was sociable, competitive and fun-loving – but also deeply religious. His father was a farmer, and the family lived a comfortable life. His mother would often read from the *Lives of Saints* to the children. Little wonder then, that four out of her eight children, dedicated their lives to Jesus.

Joseph had a strong athletic body. He was intelligent, but had no interest in formal education. He was a sensitive, compassionate boy. One day, he saw an old woman, shedding bitter tears over a cow lying seriously ill. Upon enquiry, Joseph learnt that a Veterinary doctor had been called to attend to the cow – but had opined that nothing could be done to save the animal.

When Joseph heard that the old woman's livelihood depended on the milk of the cow which she sold in the market, his heart was moved. He met the old woman and said to her, "Don't worry, mother! We will do something to help you."

He asked her to boil a concoction of herbs for the sick animal. When the concoction was ready, he administered it to the cow. He then told the old lady to rest for sometime, while he attended to the cow.

"Get well, dear cow," he said to the animal, again and again, as he kept stroking it with tender, loving care, "Your owner needs you; she depends on you!"

He prayed, cajoled, stroked the cow and administered the herbal medicine – and nursed the cow back to health! Kindness, compassion and love, were some of the important elements of Joseph's nature.

There were frequent breaks in his studies – but he resumed his education each time with fervour and enthusiasm, for it was his dream to dedicate his life to the Lord.

Joseph was hot-tempered, and would often give vent to his anger. However, he did his best to control his temper and to hold his tongue. To improve himself, he kept a reminder in front of him, upon his desk. The words, *"Silence – Recollection – Prayer,"* were carved on his desk, to remind him to control his temper.

Joseph followed his elder brother to enter the Congregation of the Sacred Hearts of Jesus and Mary, taking the habit on February 2, 1858, when he was barely 18 years old. Along with the habit, he took the religious name of Brother Damien.

His superiors in the Congregation were, at first, a little reluctant to permit him to enter priesthood. They felt he lacked proper education – especially knowledge of Latin and Greek. But such was Damien's religious fervour that he applied himself to the task before him, clearing the required tests in the classical languages to become eligible for priesthood.

As a novice, Damien would pray everyday before the picture of St. Francis Xavier, the Patron Saint of Missionaries. It was his dream to be sent out on missionary work.

In 1863, his brother was given a missionary assignment and posted to the islands of Hawaii; but he fell ill just before his departure. Damien begged his superiors to be allowed to take his brother's place, even though he had not yet been ordained as a priest. The permission was granted, and Damien arrived in Honolulu, after a five-month voyage, on March 19, 1864.

The scattered volcanic islands of Hawaii were to be Father Damien's *karma bhoomi*. He travelled tirelessly over the rough terrain of the islands, to minister to his scattered flock.

Once, a Hawaiian asked him, "Where do you live, Father?"

Damien pointed to the saddle of his horse and replied with a smile, "At present, this is my home!"

Hawaii was, at that time, an independent kingdom under a sovereign ruler. The natives of Hawaii were badly afflicted by leprosy, which had assumed epidemic proportions. In the interest of public health, the leprosy victims had to be segregated, so that the supposedly contagious disease did not spread further.

In those days, several misconceptions prevailed about leprosy. It was thought to be a curse of God; people mistakenly believed that it afflicted immoral people who were guilty of sexual misconduct. Lepers were treated as social outcasts and the Hawaiian king passed a law that all lepers must be deported to the island of Molokai.

Truly, Molokai was like a hell on earth! It was a place where people came to die. Cut off from the rest of the world, desperate, forlorn, lacking medical aid and all human comfort, the lepers lived in misery till the disease finally destroyed them. If they lacked every form of comfort in life, death was no better: they did not even have proper burial facilities, and rotting corpses littered a part of the island.

It was said that no one who entered Molokai, ever left it alive!

Father Damien volunteered to serve in Molokai.

His friends were shocked. "Don't be *mad*, Damien!" they said to him. "If you live amidst those lepers, you are sure to catch the loathsome disease yourself! And be warned – leprosy will lead to ugly deformation, torturing pain and a slow death. Once you go there, there will be no coming back! Think of the long and lonely years you will have to spend – friendless, forsaken, forlorn – till a slow, tortuous death comes to end your life!"

The desperate warnings fell on deaf ears. Father Damien had made up his mind. On May 10, 1873, he became the first Roman Catholic Priest to volunteer for service in Molokai.

The isolated segregation settlement was in a terrible condition. Apart from death and disease, lawlessness and immorality were rampant in the island forsaken by God and man! Father Damien was shocked by the sight that greeted him: desperate, aggressive, abandoned lepers; fetid odour everywhere: disfigured forms and faces; and men and women covered with infected sores, oozing pus.

Father Damien was not only physically strong; he also had emotional resilience and, above all, the strength of his religious faith. He set out to work single-handedly, to improve the life of the lepers on this island of death.

He did not receive a warm welcome from the lepers either: they were not delighted to see a man of God who had chosen to live and work with them. They stared at him in sullen suspicion.

Father Damien was not put off by their hostility. He sought to behold the image of God in them. He did not pity them because they were lepers; rather, he loved them because they were children of God. And, it did not take him long to find his way into their hearts, to convince them that he was their brother, who had come to share their burdens, care for them and comfort them and draw them closer to God.

His love and compassion worked wonders. Is not love itself, a great miracle-worker? Is not compassion the key which can open any heart? A new change swept over the leper colony. A new hope dawned in the lives of the lepers. Molokai was not just a place to die; it was a place to *live*.

"Father Damien loves us," the lepers said to each other. "For our sake, this holy man of God has come to live and work amongst us. We too, shall love him, and do whatever he asks of us."

Father Damien had a genius for organisation. He was not afraid of hard work. He began a massive task of construction on the island: eventually, he raised over 370 buildings on the island, with the help of his leper friends: these included homes, schools, orphanages, even a brand new Church – St. Philomena's – where they could gather for services and prayer.

Father Damien worked silently. He sought no publicity, no applause either from the inmates or from the outside world. All he wanted was a fellow-priest to whom he could make his confession. Periodically, a priest was sent out by the Church; but this priest remained on a boat, at a distance from the island, while Father Damien shouted his confession to him from the seashore, across the waves!

The Queen of Hawaii learnt of the noble work Father Damien was carrying out on the island. She decided to bestow the Royal Order on him. The Princess who came in person to present the red and gold cross to him, could not make her formal speech; she broke down and wept at what she saw.

As for Father Damien, he hardly wore the red and gold cross. "I did not come to Molokai for this," was his only response.

Father Damien's letters to his family began to appear in European newspapers, and the world gradually came to know of his noble work. But Father Damien shunned publicity. "I want to remain unknown to the world," he insisted.

Blessed are they who love to remain unknown to the world – who live a hidden life in the hidden God. They are truly close to the Lord!

For twelve long years, he served the lepers ceaselessly, tirelessly. His life was one of dedication, devotion and selfless sacrifice. He looked after their material needs; he nursed them in sickness; he comforted them in despair; he bathed and bandaged their sores; he carried heavy logs on his shoulders; he toiled and laboured and built homes for them; he even dug their graves!

At the end of twelve years, when he returned home one evening, exhausted, and put his feet in a basin of hot water, as was his custom, he felt no sensation.

Father Damien had contracted leprosy. He was now truly one of his flock. Like his brothers and sisters on Molokai, he too, was a leper!

He redoubled his efforts, for he knew now that he had not long to live.

By now, financial aid and medical help poured into Molokai; what is more, dedicated volunteers, nuns and priests joined Father Damien, to assist him in his chosen work. Molokai had become a model for leprosy care and rehabilitation.

On April 15, 1889, at the age of forty-nine, this holy man of Hawaii breathed his last. His brothers, the lepers, gathered around his bed in tears. The Catholic priests who were praying by his bedside, beseeched him, "Leave us your holy mantle, Revered Father!"

"What will you do with it?" Father Damien replied, "It is full of leprosy."

Damien died as he had lived, with the Name of God upon his lips, his heart and soul dedicated to God.

But Damien lives on, in the hearts of those afflicted, reviled and segregated from humanity.

Today, the world hails him as the Patron Saint of infectious, incurable diseases. And the great spirit of his selfless service lives in the minds of all dedicated volunteers who choose the life of selfless service to suffering humanity.

Sayings of Father Damien

"The Lord decorated me with His own particular cross—leprosy."

* * * * *

"Be severe toward yourself, indulgent toward others. Have scrupulous exactitude for everything regarding God: prayer, meditation, mass, administration of the Sacraments. Unite your heart with God.... Remember always your three vows, by which you are dead to the things of the world. Remember always that God is eternal and work courageously in order one day to be united with Him forever."

Some Books on Father Damien

- *Holy Man: Father Damien of Molokai* – by Gavan Daws
- *Leper Priest of Molokai: The Father Damien Story* – by Richard Stewart
- *Father Damien And The Bells* – by Elizabeth Odell Sheehan
- *Father Damien: The Man Who Lived and Died for the Victims of Leprosy (People Who Have Helped the World)* – by Pam Brown
- *Molokai: The Story of Father Damien* – by Hilde Eynikel
- *Damien the Leper* – by John Farrow

Hasan Darvesh

Hasan Darvesh was a Sufi Saint – a true lover of God. Rejecting wealth, power and fame, he dedicated his life to a search for the Truth – the Truth that he shared with aspiring souls who came to sit at his feet. Hassan taught that the secret of the Life Beautiful lay in three things – perseverance, effort and renunciation.

Hasan Darvesh

Humanity has indeed, been blessed by the wealth of true wisdom and grace bestowed on us by Sufi Saints. They were true lovers of God. They wanted nothing for themselves – neither wealth, nor name, nor fame, nor the luxuries of this world. From the innermost recesses of their hearts, they exclaimed: "We want Thee and only Thee, Beloved! We need nothing besides!" For them, nothing existed, nothing mattered, apart from the love of the Lord!

One of them was Hasan – reverently called Hazrat Hasan-al Basri. In his early life, before the call came to him, he was a reputed jeweller, dealing in precious stones. He carried on business with kings, princes and rich folk. Then, he went through an experience that transformed him and awakened his soul. He became famous as a mystic whose name is now closely associated with that of Rabia. Both these saints represent early Sufism. A shining star in asceticism and devotion to God, Hasan is revered for his dedication to truth, and his deep knowledge of the Divine.

When he was a child, we are told, he was fortunate to drink the water that was left in the cup from which Prophet Muhammed had drank. When this was brought to the notice of Prophet Muhammed, he remarked: "This child will receive from the Lord a quantum of spiritual knowledge to match to the water he drank."

The word "hasan" means "the beautiful". And Hasan was indeed truly beautiful.

We are given a fascinating story of how the call came to this great mystic. It happened thus.

One day, he went on a business-trip to Rum, and stayed with the Minister of the Sultan.

The Minister told him that he was accompanying the Sultan on an important mission and invited Hasan to join the company. Hasan gladly agreed to do so. The caravan of the Sultan departed, Hasan accompanying them. They arrived at a lonely place where they pitched a magnificent tent. The tent was heavily guarded.

First, the army officers entered the tent and came out in a few minutes. They were followed by a few distinguished citizens, who like the military officers, entered the tent, uttered a few lines and came out. This was followed by medical experts who went through the same procedure. Then came two hundred extremely beautiful maidens who also did likewise. Lastly, the Sultan accompanied by his ministers entered the tent, uttered a few lines, circumambulated the tent and came out.

Surprised at the incident, Hasan enquired of the Minister what all of this meant. He was told that a very handsome and brave young son of the Sultan had died a few years earlier. His body was buried in the tomb, at this lonely spot, over which the tent had been erected. Every year, as a mark of respect, the Sultan visited the tomb and performed the ceremony, which Hasan had just witnessed.

At first the army officers would address the prince and say to him, "O Prince, if by our arms and weapons we could have saved thee from the clutches of death, we would have gladly sacrificed our lives to save your life. But, before the God of Death our strength and valour were useless."

Then came the learned citizens who said, "O Prince, if our knowledge, wisdom and experience could have saved thee, we would have averted your death, but before the God of Death our wisdom and expertise were useless."

Then came the doctors who also said, "If our medicines could have saved thee, we would have left no stone unturned, but, before the God of Death our skills were futile."

Then came the beautiful maidens who said, "If our beauty could have saved you, we would have sacrificed our all – but we were powerless before the God of Death."

Finally, came the Sultan who said, "My son! My ministers, my maidens, my doctors, my citizens, my army, my wealth, my power, none of these could stop the inevitable. Before the God of Death all of us were helpless. We now bid you good bye and will visit you again next year."

This incident left an indelible impression on the heart of Hasan. He kept asking himself, if death is, indeed, the end of life, have I made any preparation for this long, inevitable journey?

He realised that death does not differentiate between the commoner and the noble, the rich and the poor, the intellectual and the illiterate. It just extinguishes life indiscriminately and heartlessly.

Hasan returned to Basra and gave up his business. He renounced everything and started upon his quest. He felt that he had only one need – and that was God.

One day, he was seated on the bank of a river when his eyes fell on a man sitting beside a woman, a jar of wine between the two of them. He thought to himself, how could these two waste their life in such idle pursuits? Just then a boat that was sailing on the river, capsized all of a sudden. The man immediately jumped into the water and tried valiantly, to rescue the seven men who were thrown out of the boat.

With great difficulty he managed to rescue six of them. Then, turning towards Hasan, he said, "If you consider yourself as a holy man, superior to the rest of us, you could at least try to save the seventh man."

Hasan felt embarrassed. The man continued, "This lady that you see by me is my mother, and this jar contains pure water."

Hasan immediately fell down at his feet and cried, "Just as you saved those six people from drowning, have mercy on me, too, and save me from drowning in the waters of egoism and pride."

The man lifted up Hasan and embraced him and said, "May God fulfill your desire!"

Hasan would sometimes write his sins on the garments he wore and would often read them in the course of the day. Sometimes, he would shed unbidden tears of repentance for the sins he had committed. He considered himself inferior to all. Is this not the one essential mark of a true man of God? He becomes humble as ashes and dust.

As Hasan grew in reflection and insight, he began to talk to people, to share his wisdom with others. His sermons touched the hearts of the listeners. He preached every Friday. Even Rabia, a great mystic herself, regularly attended his sermons. Great was the reverence Hasan had for Rabia. One day, Rabia was late in coming to his fellowship assembly. Hasan would not start his sermon. He waited for Rabia to arrive. One of those present at the meeting asked him, "Sir, why do you wait for Rabia? There are so many people eagerly waiting to listen to your sermon." Hasan answered, "Whatever light shineth in my words cometh to me from the heart of Rabia."

The last day of his life arrived. As Hasan lay on his sick bed, surrounded by his disciples, he said to them, "It is time for me to depart and bid you goodbye."

A disciple said to Him, "In your grace, you have told us several things about yourself, but you have never revealed to us who your *murshid* or Guru was. At whose Lotus Feet did you receive the true knowledge of the spirit?"

"I have had three Gurus," he answered. "It is from these three that I learnt the true lessons of life."

The Saint continued, "The first Guru was a thief, the second, a child and the third, a dog."

The disciples were astonished as they heard those words. "How could a thief be a Guru?" they enquired.

Upon this, Hasan answered, "I observed many spiritual disciplines, I lived a life of intense austerity, I put my body through torture, but I gained nothing. Then, one day, in dismay, I said to myself, "Perhaps, this spiritual path, this life of austerity is not meant for me! Before I stepped on the spiritual path, I lived a life of pomp and pleasure, I was a successful jeweller who sold jewels to kings and emperors. I said to myself "Now that I have renounced everything and am trying to tread the spiritual path, I seem to have achieved nothing!"

Immersed in those thoughts, Hasan said, he reached a village. It was midnight. He looked around the village, but there was darkness everywhere. After a while, a person emerged from one of the cottages.

Hasan went up to him and said, "Brother, I am a pilgrim. I do not know anyone here. It would be nice if I could find a place in which to spend the night. There is darkness all around. Everyone seems to be asleep. You are the only one who is awake. Please tell me, who you are and may I stay in your cottage tonight?"

The stranger said to Hasan, "Sir, you appear to be a holy man of God. But, may I tell you, who I am? I am a thief. In the middle of the night I leave my house, because my work begins when the people are asleep."

The thief continued, "At night I step out, and go to plunder and rob. People tremble on hearing my name."

When Hasan heard those words, he thought to himself, "This man is so honest and transparent. He is not hiding anything from me. He is telling me the truth about himself!"

The thief continued, "My cottage is empty. If you wish, you can spend the night there. People are so frightened of me, they do not even come near my hut. So, if you wish, you can spend, not just one night, but as many nights as you desire in my humble abode."

Hasan Darvesh spent the night in the thief's cottage. In the dark of the dawn, the thief returned. On his face was a smile.

Hasan asked him, "Brother, did you succeed in getting anything at night?"

"No!" replied the thief, "I did not get a chance to break into any house. However, I did try my best."

Hasan continued to stay in the thief's cottage for several days. He noticed that whether the thief brought anything home or not, there was always a smile on his face. This went on, night after night. A whole month passed. Hasan then realised that God was teaching him a lesson through the thief. The thief was engaged in acquiring material wealth, but was not discouraged by failure. And yet, he did not give up his efforts.

Hasan said to himself: "I am trying to acquire the treasure which is not of this world, the treasure which is far richer and nobler than all the wealth of this world, but I get depressed and dejected at not being successful in my efforts! I say to myself, I have done a lot of *sadhana* (self-discipline), *tapasya* (austerity) and put in so much effort, but have not achieved anything. I feel like giving up! The thief has taught me a great lesson."

The thief thus became Hasan's first Guru. He taught Hasan never, never, never to give up but to keep on striving until the goal is reached!

"My second Guru," Hasan continued, "was a child."

One day, a child passed in front of Hasan, with a lighted lamp in his hand. Hasan asked him, "O my sweet child, who has lit this lamp that you are carrying? Where did the light come from?"

Hearing this, the child immediately blew out the flame. Then he asked Hasan, "Tell me where did the light go? You asked me where did the light come from; first tell me, where did the light go?"

The child continued further, "In this lamp, there is a cotton wick and there is oil too. There is a matchbox in my hands. But still the wick cannot be lit. The wick can only be lit when I take a matchstick and strike it against the match box. The flame thus created, will ignite the cotton and the wick will be lit."

Hearing all this from the little child's lips, Hasan was astonished. "Tell me, my dear," he said to the child, "how did you acquire all this knowledge and wisdom?"

The child replied, "My father spends a lot of time with saints and holy people like you. Those saints taught my father many things and my father has passed on this knowledge to me."

Hasan Darvesh learnt from this child, that all of us have been given cotton, oil and a matchbox as well. God has endowed us with these three gifts. We just have to strike the matchbox, ignite the wick and obtain the flame. Everything is with us already. We do not have to go anywhere in search of anything. Some people travel long distances to go on pilgrimages. It all seems so futile, when what we desire in this world has already been given to us. We just have to light the lamp.

His third Guru, Hasan said, was a dog. One day when Hasan stood near a river, he saw a dog. The dog was out of breath. He seemed to be very thirsty, and his tongue was hanging out. Before the dog was the river, with its flowing waters. The weather was sultry and the river water was cool. The dog's thirst drew him to the river. But as soon as he bent his head to drink water, he saw his own reflection in it. He thought it was another dog in the water. This frightened him, and he at once withdrew. His intense thirst made him feel miserable. He bent down once again to slake his thirst, but his own image reflected in the water petrified him. This was repeated for the third time. Finally, the dog was overpowered by thirst and jumped into the water. This created ripples, which did not allow him to see his own reflection in the water: and he drank the water to his heart's content.

The Darvesh said, "This dog taught me that in this jealous world, many people seek happiness, but for some reason or the other, are unable to drink the waters of joy and happiness." We come close to divine peace and joy but are unable to partake of it and satiate our thirst. If we wish to slake our thirst, we should be prepared to jump into the waters. Jumping means forgetting everything else, leaving all else behind.

Such was the wisdom of Hasan *darvesh,* who taught us the valuable lessons of perseverance, effort and renunciation. Every person he met, every incident and accident which befell him, was a source of wisdom and inspiration to him. He practised true renunciation – which was not just external, but an inner experience to him. And he never, ever, lost sight of the one unchanging truth of life – that we come into this world, alone; and that we will have to depart from this world, alone.

Mother Teresa

Mother Teresa was a living, moving picture of the teaching enshrined in the Sermon on the Mount. Her life bore witness to the fact that the Sermon on the Mount is not a mere vision of a seer but a profound reality in practical life. Frail and wrinkled with age, Mother Teresa continued to work on, till her last breath, in sunshine and rain, in adversity and amidst opposition, as a servant of the poor. She was blessed with the strength of ten, because in her heart was love, and every fibre of her being thrilled with faith in the living Lord. She tended the terminally sick and nursed the handicapped, the lonely and the lost. She served the poorest of the poor, the unwanted and unloved, beholding in them pictures of God. For her, indeed, to serve the poor was to worship God.

Mother Teresa

Sri Krishna was once asked, "You are called by a myriad Names. Tell us, which is the Name dearest to your heart?"

Sri Krishna smiled a dazzling smile and said, "Call me by my favourite name – *Daridra Narayana* – for, I am the friend of those whom this world tramples upon and treats as dirt." He added, "If you truly wish to worship Me, go and serve the friendless, the forsaken and the forlorn, with love and devotion in your hearts, for whatever you offer to them in love, it is as though you have offered it to Me!"

And Jesus said, "Whatever you do to the least of the little ones, that you verily do unto Me!"

Mother Teresa, did exactly that – she served the homeless, the destitute, the dying, the forsaken and forlorn – she called them the unwanted and the unloved – with utter love and devotion. She made selfless service the goal of her life. She gathered to her heart those from whom the world turned away in proud disdain. She came to be known as 'The Saint of the Gutters'.

Born on August 27, 1910, in Skopje, Macedonia, she was the youngest of three children born to Nicholle and Drandafille Bojaxhiu, and her parents gave her the name, Agnes. Her father was a successful and well-known contractor; her mother, a simple housewife. They were pious Roman Catholics and went to Church regularly. They shared what they could with the poor and needy.

We are told, that the mother took care of a woman who was an alcoholic, and tried her best to rehabilitate her. The child, Agnes, as she grew in years, learnt the lessons of caring and sharing from her parents. From them, too, she imbibed the spirit of serving the unloved and the unwanted.

As a young girl, Agnes was fond of reading books and singing songs. She was a member of the Church Choir.

In 1919, when Agnes was barely nine years of age, her father passed away, and the burden of raising the family fell on the mother. To make ends meet, the pious mother took to stitching and embroidering wedding dresses – and thus life went on, for the family.

Young Agnes was filled with a strong urge to be of service to suffering humanity. Her heart moved out to the poor and needy and she looked for opportunities to care for them. Her spiritual quest took her to a Father Confessor, the local parish priest, to whom she spoke of her inner urge. "Do you think

I am fit for a life of dedication to the Lord?" she asked him, in all earnestness.

"Let your inner joy be the criteria for your decision," the priest advised her. "The joy you feel in the heart will indicate to you, the direction your life should take."

Indeed, her heart led Agnes in the right direction. In 1928, she entered the *Order of The Sisters of Our Lady of Loretto*. She received religious training in Dublin and was then sent to a dream destination – India. For this was the country she had chosen to serve!

In Calcutta, where she was posted, she became a teacher at St. Mary's High School, where she taught geography and catechism, rising soon to the position of Principal. However, in 1946, she fell seriously ill, and was unable to continue teaching. Her convent sent her to Darjeeling for convalescence. On her way to Darjeeling, on the 10th of September, she said, she received a calling from God, "to serve Him among the poorest of the poor." Teresa responded to the call, and requested her convent to relieve her of her duties and permit her to establish her own order of sisters. However, the Archbishop of Calcutta requested her to continue her teaching assignment in the convent for a year longer.

At the end of the year, Teresa renewed her request to start her own order. It was another year before the official permission was granted by the Vatican and, in 1948, Teresa started her new order. The sisters of her order had their own 'habit'. It was chosen by Teresa – a simple white saree with a blue border, distinctly Indian in form and spirit. Clad in her white saree, Teresa set out on her mission. No one knew her; no one even recognised the former Principal of St. Mary's School. She had just five rupees with her; and she said to herself, "Teresa can do very little with five rupees, but God and Teresa can do a lot with the paltry sum!"

Teresa chose to begin her work in the slum behind St. Mary's School, where she had taught poor children earlier. The slum was filthy and foul-smelling, and the slum dwellers were victims of several diseases. Teresa taught them basic hygiene and taught them to keep themselves and their surroundings clean. She also continued to teach the poor children to read and write.

Some of Teresa's friends were eager to join her new order. The first one to seek her out was a former student, Sister Agnes, a Bengali girl from a well-to-do family, who came to stay with her and assist her.

Teresa explained to her patiently that it was a tough life she had chosen: she asked the girl to rethink her decision and then take the final step. But the girl was quite firm in her resolve, and decided to join Teresa. Other sisters followed suit.

In their small and humble Home, the little Sisters of the Poor led an austere and dedicated life. They woke up early in the morning to begin their day with

Prayer and Communion – for Teresa was of the firm belief that it was only through prayer that they would receive faith and strength.

Homeless old folk, abandoned babies found in rubbish-heaps and sore-infested lepers were brought to the sisters for help, healing and support – and each one was received with abundant love and kindness. The number of sisters gradually increased. It was clear that they needed a larger Home where they could all live together with the poor who depended on them. But they had no money to buy or rent such a property! How could they procure the needed funds? Who would offer them the help and support they needed?

Unfortunately, there were enough and more people to discourage them. Instead of offering support, several people heaped scorn on them.

One gentleman came to meet Teresa and said to her, "I have a large house to offer you. Come and take a look at it. I will sell it to you at a low price."

The sisters went to see his house, but it was very old and dilapidated. It looked as if the roof and walls would collapse any minute! Mother Teresa shook her head in despair and said to the man, "How can we live in such a house?"

"No, no!" the man exclaimed. "You misjudge the house! See how strong it is!" And to prove his point, he banged on the wall beside him. Immediately, the wall crashed and the roof collapsed!

Undaunted, Mother Teresa and her team continued their search and in a short while, they managed to find a property which suited their needs.

The sisters who joined Mother Teresa had to take four vows:

1. Firstly, the vow of Poverty, which meant that they would possess *nothing*. Nothing belonged to them: everything belonged to the Lord.
2. Secondly, the vow of Chastity, which enjoined purity of thought, word and deed.
3. Thirdly, the vow of Obedience, which implied that they would, without question, do as they were asked to do.
4. Fourthly, the vow of Charity, which meant that their entire life was an offering to God.

It was a tough life – but judged in terms of Mother Teresa's Father Confessor – it was a life of deep inner joy. Every morning, the sisters would arise at 4:00 a.m. and spend some time in prayer and meditation. Then they would get ready to serve the poor and the needy.

One day, as Mother Teresa was walking down the road, she saw something moving in a dirty ditch. Drawing closer, she was horrified to see that it was a sick woman, groaning in pain. Rats were scurrying over her inert body, some of them even nibbling at her face and limbs. She lay there in the filth and dirt, unable to move, powerless to drive away the pests and rodents crawling all over her. Truly, she was in a pathetic and miserable condition! Mother Teresa was moved to tears. With tear-touched eyes, she lifted the woman out of the ditch and had her carried to a hospital. However, the hospital authorities refused to admit her, as she had no address. Mother Teresa rushed from one hospital to another, with the ailing woman, but all to no avail. The woman breathed her last in Mother's arms!

This incident moved Mother Teresa profoundly. She resolved then and there, that she would found an institution where such the poor, unwanted, uncared for people could live their last days of life peacefully, and die with grace and dignity.

With this thought, she approached the Kolkata Municipal Corporation and requested them to allot a place where she could set up such a Home.

The Corporation officials, at first, were not prepared to respond to her request. But after some persuasion, they showed her a place behind a Kali Temple in the city. At one time, it had been a guest house for visitors to the city. But now it had been reduced to a place of disrepute, frequented by drunkards, gamblers and drug addicts. The Corporation officials told her very magnanimously that the rundown building was of no use to them now, and that she could have it if she wanted it.

Mother Teresa visited the place with one of her sisters, only to be confronted by a bunch of drunkards and drug addicts. They threw stones at the sisters, shouting at them and warning them to go away, for they needed the place for their own use, especially during nights, when they congregated there.

Surmounting many such threats and obstacles, Mother Teresa carried on her work of help and healing. Some people once complained to the police that she should not be provided space to carry on her work, as she gathered 'unsavoury' people around her. A lady police commissioner was sent to make a surprise check on Mother Teresa's Home. Do you know what the Officer found?

She saw Mother Teresa attending to a dying man. His body was covered with oozing pores, and maggot-infested sores. Mother was cleansing his wounds with her own hands; tears streamed down her cheeks, even as she murmured a prayer to God to heal the ailing brother.

The Police Commissioner's heart melted at the sight. She promised Mother Teresa that she would do whatever lay within her power to enable her to carry on her mission of help and healing.

Mother Teresa's Mission was, as she mentioned when she accepted the Nobel Prize, "to care for the hungry, the naked, the homeless, the crippled, the blind, the lepers, all those people who feel unwanted, unloved, uncared for throughout society, people that have become a burden to the society and are shunned by everyone."

Mother Teresa's new Home was located just behind a Kali Temple. One day, the temple priest contracted cholera, and no one was prepared to look after him. He lay helpless and abandoned on the road, outside the temple. Mother Teresa happened to see him as she was passing by. Immediately, she had him picked up and carried to her Home where he was looked after with tender, loving care by the sisters, and nursed back to good health.

Even as she was totally immersed in her life of service, Mother Teresa was aware that people shunned lepers and the dying destitutes, virtually turning their faces and running away from them. Then there were young, unwed mothers, who wanted to abandon their newborn children, and left them in garbage bins. Mother Teresa included all of them in her loving care. She opened a separate shelter for orphaned children, and sent messages to local hospitals to send their unwanted babies to her. "I will take care of them," she promised. "I shall fight abortion with adoption."

Many newborn babies were brought to her, some of them undernourished, weak, feeble, weighing less than a kilo. Quite a few of them did not survive – but those who did, were cared for with love and affection by the Mother and her team. Mother would encourage families to adopt those children so that they would have someone to care for them.

During a few decades of dedicated work, Mother Teresa accomplished a great deal. She established colonies for lepers, homes for the homeless and institutions to care for orphans. In the year 1979, she was awarded the prestigious Nobel Peace Prize.

It is a tradition to host a grand banquet in honour of a Nobel Laureate. Mother Teresa declined the invitation and told the organisers, "Please hand over the entire sum to me, so that I can provide food and medical aid to hundreds of thousands of my poor brothers and sisters in India."

Accepting the Nobel Peace Prize, Mother Teresa observed quite simply, that when we reach the end of our earthly pilgrimage, we will not be judged by our degrees and diplomas, or by the wealth we have accumulated. Only one thing would matter then: the service that we have rendered to those who need it most; the care and compassion we have offered to the unwanted and unloved.

How true are Mother Teresa's words!

I had the privilege of meeting Mother Teresa for the first time in Oxford, where we had been invited to attend a Conference of Spiritual and Parliamentary Leaders. When she came to the podium to address the delegates, she was so tiny that she was completely hidden by the podium, and nobody could see her. The organisers made her stand on a small stool so that she could be visible to the distinguished audience. To them she gave the same message: "We are here to help the helpless, the forsaken and forlorn, the unwanted and unloved. The day on which we have not helped someone in need is a lost day, indeed!"

Every morning, as we awaken to a new day, let us remember her message. Every morning, let us ask ourselves: What can I do to help others? How can I ease the pain and suffering of others? For, indeed, each one of us can and must make a difference – or else, we would have lived this life in vain!

Recently, a book has been published which reveals that Mother Teresa had persistently tried and failed to feel the presence of God during more than 50 years of her life, and consequently felt "lost and empty". In her darkest moments, she came perilously close to doubting whether God really existed or not. She felt she had become "trapped in Hell" as she did her work among the destitute and the dying.

In private letters that Mother Teresa wrote, she insisted that she should be cremated after her death, but the Vatican ordered otherwise; Mother Teresa also describes the "darkness, loneliness and torture", she constantly felt which made her doubt the very existence of Heaven and God.

In a letter to Father Michael van der Peet, a spiritual adviser and close confidant, Mother Teresa writes: "Jesus has a very special love for you. But as for me, the silence and emptiness is so great that I look and do not see, listen and do not hear, the tongue moves but does not speak. I want you to pray for me – that I let Him have a free hand."

We are told that Mother Teresa continued to work among the destitute and the dying with a smile on her face, though her mind was in a state of turmoil. She even said that her life was one of almost constant "torture" and that her smile "was a mask – a cloak that covers everything."

Mysterious, most mysterious are the ways of God. And I have no doubt that on September 5, 1997, when she dropped her physical body, Jesus came to take her in his loving arms. He must have whispered in her ears something like: "Welcome, My child, here am I to receive you. You worked, you toiled, you laboured – all for My sake, without getting a single response from Me. But you did not give up! You passed through the fire of suffering, loneliness, rejection. You have come out of it shining, radiant as thrice-burnished gold. Kudos to you!"

In life as in death, Mother Teresa was an Angel of Mercy.

Let us bow down our heads in humble tribute to this holy woman who adopted our country as her own! Let us try to do at least, one good act of service everyday, in her sacred memory!

Sayings of Mother Teresa

"Every time you smile at someone, it is an action of love, a gift to that person, a beautiful thing."

* * * * *

"God doesn't require us to succeed; He only requires that we try."

* * * * *

"Good works are links that form a chain of love."

* * * * *

"If we have no peace, it is because we have forgotten that we belong to each other."

* * * * *

"If you judge people, you have no time to love them. If you want a love message to be heard, it has got to be sent out. To keep a lamp burning, we have to keep putting oil in it."

* * * * *

"Kind words can be short and easy to speak, but their echoes are truly endless."

* * * * *

I do not pray for success, I ask for faithfulness.

* * * * *

I have found the paradox, that if you love until it hurts, there can be no more hurt, only more love.

* * * * *

I know God will not give me anything I can't handle. I just wish that He didn't trust me so much.

Some Books by Mother Teresa

- *In My Own Words* – Mother Teresa, Compiled by José Luis Gonzales-Balado
- *The Blessings of Love* – Mother Teresa, Selected and Edited by Nancy Sabbag
- *Thirsting for God*
- *Love: A Fruit Always in Season: Daily Meditations*
- *Meditations from a Simple Path*
- *Seeking the Heart of God: Reflections on Prayer*

Some Books on Mother Teresa

- *Mother Teresa: A Complete Authorized Biography* – by Kathryn Spink
- *Mother Teresa* – by Demi (Illustrator)
- *Mother Teresa: In the Shadow of Our Lady* – by Joseph Langford
- *Mother Teresa's Prescription: Finding Happiness And Peace in Service* – by Paul A., M.D. Wright
- *Life with Mother Teresa: My Thirty-year Friendship With The Mother of The Poor* – by Sebastian Vazhakala
- *Mother Teresa: Friend to the Poor* (Childhood of World Figures) – by Kathleen Kudlinski
- *Mother Teresa's Lessons of Love and Secrets of Sanctity* – by Susan Conroy
- *Come Be My Light* – by Brian Kolodiejchuk, M.C.
- *Works of Love Are Works of Peace: Mother Teresa of Calcutta and the Missionaries of Charity* – by Michael Collopy and Mother Teresa

Ishadassi

*I*shadassi was a great *sadhvi* who accepted sorrow and suffering as a gift from God. An aspiring soul who sought to dedicate her life to God, she was forced again, and again, into a life of bondage, a life that tied her to fickle human relationships. Hurt and rejected repeatedly, she still stood firm in her faith and unquestioning acceptance of the Will Divine, until she found the Light she had sought all her life. She herself became a transmitter of this Light for the benefit of others. She was truly a servant of God.

Ishadassi

A little girl met me after the evening *satsang*. Her eyes gleaming, she asked me if she could become a *yogini*, a holy woman. I said to her, "My child, you can only try and put in your best efforts. But to really become a true *sadhvi*, a *yogini* or a holy person, is not in the hands of an individual. You can become a *sadhvi* or a *yogini* only by the Grace of God. You can put forth your best efforts and keep on praying to God for it, but it will happen only if He Wills it."

Innocently, the girl continued, "Whenever I express this desire to my parents, they tell me to discard such ideas. 'If you become a *yogini*, you will have to face many obstacles, and bear many hardships,' they say to me. Is it true that all who have become sages, saints and great souls have had to face tremendous difficulties and problems?"

I answered, "My child, some people easily become saints or *sadhvis*, but there are others who have to face many obstacles, many trials before they can become holy men or women. However, all saints and *sadhvis* regard every experience that comes to them – pleasant or unpleasant, bitter or sweet – as God's *prasadam*. On their lips are the words:

> Thou knowest everything, Beloved!
>   Let Thy Will always be done!
> In joy and sorrow, my Beloved!
>   Let Thy Will always be done!

"Could you please tell me of such an one – a *sadhvi*, who had accepted sorrow and suffering as a gift of God?" the girl asked.

"Gladly," I said to her. And I spoke to her of a holy woman. Her name was Ishadassi. The meaning of the word *dassi* is servant and this *sadhvi*, Ishadassi, was truly a servant of God.

Ishadassi was born in Ujjain. Her father was a businessman and her mother was a woman of noble qualities. Ishadassi was the only child of her parents. They both loved their daughter very much and took great care of her.

Since her early childhood, Ishadassi had this one desire, that she might offer her entire life at the feet of the Lord; that she might not get enmeshed in this world of unreality and unrest. Once, she learnt that a holy man had come to visit her town. She went to have his *darshan* and blessings. She joined in the *kirtan* sessions and, at times, went into a trance.

As Ishadassi grew in years, she became more and more beautiful. It was even said of her: "Ishadassi is like a rose without thorns!"

One day, a rich businessman from Sialkot, visited their house. He saw the young beauty and said to himself, "She is so good-natured and so beautiful. She serves everyone and has a radiant smile on her face, all the time. Why don't I get her married to my son?"

The wealthy man took an instant liking to Ishadassi. He approached her father and said, "This daughter of yours is not only beautiful but is also endowed with wonderful qualities of culture and character. I wish to offer my son in marriage to her."

The parents were thrilled. They pressed Ishadassi to accept the offer. Obviously, she did not wish to enter a matrimonial alliance, for she had wished to dedicate her life to the Lord. However, she could not disobey her parents and the marriage was soon solemnised.

Ishadassi left the town of Ujjain and came to live in Sialkot. Every morning, she would wake up early and bow down at the feet of her father-in-law and mother-in-law. She would take their blessings, then go and attend to her husband. She would care for his every need. She never thought of her own comforts, but did all she could to keep her husband and in-laws happy in every way.

Strange are the ways of destiny! The husband, whom she served so faithfully, and whom she tried to please in every way, one day, turned around and told his parents, "I do not want to live here any longer. I want to go to a far-off country."

When his parents questioned him, he said, "What can I do? I do not wish to live with Ishadassi."

"Why don't you want to live with her?" the parents asked, bewildered. "She cares for you so much, she loves you tremendously. She gives you so much attention. Your least wish is a command to her. Then what is the reason for your wanting to leave her?"

The husband replied, "I just don't know! But, I am sure, I do not wish to live here."

The father and mother-in-law were nonplussed. They asked Ishadassi, "Your husband is desirous of leaving Sialkot and living in a far-off land. Did you by any chance cause offence to him in any way?"

Ishadaasi was shocked. "I have always served him and placed his happiness above my own. His every wish has been a command for me and I have always fulfilled it. My only wish is that whether I am happy or not, my dear husband should always be happy."

The parents tried very hard to make their son understand. But he was stubborn and refused to listen to them.

Finally, the mother and father requested Ishadassi, "Rather than our son leaving us and going to a distant land, it would be better if you could go back to your father's house."

"This must be the result of my *karma*," Ishadassi thought to herself, "otherwise, why would my husband want me to leave him? I had put in every effort to keep him satisfied and happy. Surely, there must be some good for me even in this bitter experience."

She left her husband and returned to her parents in Ujjain.

Her parents were very worried to see Ishadassi. In those days, it was considered wrong to have one's daughter at home. So they decided to get Ishadassi married, a second time. Much against her will, a few months later, they arranged for her marriage with the son of another rich businessman. Ishadassi served her second husband sincerely, lovingly, faithfully. For her, to live was to serve, to live was to do good to others.

Barely a month passed by, when the second husband complained, "I do not want to live with Ishadassi."

The second husband also abandoned her!

Once more, Ishadassi was back at her parents' home. Even then her faith in the Lord remained firm. "Whatever happens," she would reiterate, "is for my ultimate good."

It was true, she was very hurt. Many questions arose within her mind. "Why do these things happen to me? What is the reason behind all this?" But, she believed in Divine Providence. She believed, that every experience that came to her was just the right experience occurring at the right time, to train her in the right way.

A few more months passed by. The parents started worrying about their young daughter: "What will happen to her after we pass away? There will be no one to look after our lovely daughter!"

One day, a *sanyasi*, a hermit, knocked at the door of their house. He begged for alms. Seeing him, the father thought to himself: "This *sanyasi* is a young man. Why should I not get my daughter married to him?"

The father said to the *sanyasi*, "Give up your life as a hermit and get married to my beautiful daughter and stay in this house as my son-in-law."

And so Ishadassi was married yet again, for the *third* time.

Both the *sanyasi* and Ishadassi stayed in the house with her parents. They stayed together for fifteen days. On the sixteenth day, the *sanyasi* approached the girl's father, "I do not wish to remain here as a *grihasta* (married man). I want to live as a *sanyasi*. Kindly return my begging-bowl to me and take charge of your lovely daughter."

For the third time, this beautiful, cultured and good-natured girl was rejected. In spite of this third rejection, Ishadassi's faith was not shaken.

One day, a sage came to their town. Ishadassi's father invited the sage to come and have a meal in his house. The sage, along with his disciples, came to the house for a meal. In his discourse, he said, "Whatever occurs in our lives is the result of our *karma*. As we sow, so shall we reap. We have to put in tremendous effort to free ourselves from this wheel of *karma*, which is a wheel of suffering and pain. We have to pray to God continuously: O Lord, free us from this wheel of suffering and pain."

On hearing the touching words of the sage, Ishadassi's heart was moved. She burst out sobbing. Falling at the feet of the sage, she requested him, "Accept me at your feet as your devotee."

Ishadassi began to live in the company of the sage. She served him, she followed his teachings and, one day, by God's Grace she herself became a *sadhvi*.

She travelled from place to place, gave discourses, specially to women. She held special *satsangs* for them. She passed on to them the teaching that in whatever happens, there is a meaning of God's mercy.

Many things happen to us in the course of our lives. We cannot understand why they have happened. It is not for us to question why. Let us accept every incident and accident that happens to us with a smile and move forward – ever onward, upward, inward, Godward. Every experience – pleasant or otherwise – comes to teach us a lesson we need to learn.

This earth is not a pleasure-hunting ground. This earth is a school: and experience is our teacher. Let us not try to run away from any experience, howsoever, difficult it be. Let us move forward to greet every experience with the words: what teaching have you brought for me? If we avoid an experience, we may succeed for some time. But it will return to us, in due course, wearing a more formidable form, and we shall be compelled to accept it. For it has to teach us a lesson we need to learn. Until we have learnt the lesson, it will not leave us. The best way, therefore, to face difficult situations is to accept them and cooperate with their inner purpose, all the while fixing our mind and heart on Him who has planned for each one of us, the glorious liberty that belongs to us as children of the Lord.

May God's blessings be showered on us, so that we accept every experience and rejoice in every situation in which we are placed! Let us repeat, as often as we can, the words:

> Thou knowest everything, Beloved,
> > Let Thy Will always be done!
> In joy and sorrow, my Beloved,
> > Let Thy Will always be done!

Dr. Albert Schweitzer

Dr. Albert Schweitzer was one of history's most amazing personalities. He was a learned man who, for the love of Jesus, became a servant of the forsaken and forlorn. He was a master-musician who saw the Face of God in the neglected Africans of the Congo. The secret of Albert Schweitzer's life lay in his identification with the poorest of the poor, the depressed, the dispossessed, the downcast ones. He was a teacher of humanity, a prophet of reverence for all life, a thinker, a singer, a servant of Jesus whose heart was filled with profound love for the neglected ones.

Dr. Albert Schweitzer

Dr. Albert Schweitzer was one of history's most amazing personalities – a scholar, a gifted musician, a doctor who devoted his life to the service of the poor and neglected people – a white European who saw the image of Christ in the faces of the black people belonging to the forsaken tribes of Africa.

As a child he was forcibly escorted to the piano by his old aunt, who told the small boy, "You must not give up practising! If you really want to play well, you must burn midnight oil. You never know what you can do with your music, one day!"

The little boy took her advice to heart. He practised his music lessons tirelessly – though, at that time, neither the old aunt nor the young boy really foresaw what he would be able to accomplish with his music. The little boy, Albert Schweitzer, not only built one of the most famous hospitals in the world, but he also became a well-known musician, and used the power of his music to heal the sick and the ailing!

Truly, Dr. Albert Schweitzer was one of the most amazing personalities of the modern age – an intellectual giant and a musical genius, who chose to become a servant of the poor.

Born to affluence, he sacrificed a life of comfort and luxury to serve the black people of Africa.

Son of a pastor, Albert Schweitzer was born in Kaysersberg, Alsace, Germany, in 1875. A gentle and quiet boy, he was loved by everyone.

He was a sensitive child who learnt his lessons in life seriously. He tells us of an incident from his boyhood which left a deep impact on him. When he was out riding with his friends, he was overcome by a sudden impulse to "show off" his prowess before his friends. He whipped and spurred his horse, driving the animal at a breakneck speed. When he dismounted, he was shocked to see how drained and exhausted the horse looked. He would never ever forget that look!

On another occasion, he was riding a horse-drawn sleigh, when a vicious dog sprang at the horse's head. Wishing to protect his horse, Albert whipped the dog to drive it away. The whip lashed at the dog's eye, and the dog rolled on the snow, groaning in the agony of pain. The howls and groans of the wounded dog haunted Albert for weeks, after the incident.

Albert could not forget these incidents. The realisation dawned on him at a young age that it was a dreadful thing to cause pain. "I have no right to inflict suffering or pain on any living creature," he told himself firmly.

Albert felt he was truly blessed to have a happy family, a comfortable home, good health and good friends. He was popular and well-liked in his school and in the neighbourhood. But he did not take it all for granted. Instead, he would constantly ask himself, "What have I done to deserve this?"

The answer came to him from within: "To whom much is given, of him much is expected." Thus was laid the foundation of a life of selfless service and sacrifice.

Having obtained a doctorate in theology, Albert became a pastor, like his father. In his leisure hours, he continued to practise his music, which had always been his passion. He became a maestro, a gifted organist. He even acquired a doctorate in music, specialising in the organ, his chosen instrument.

A serious and profound scholar, it was not long before he acquired a third doctorate in philosophy. At a young age, he started teaching those subjects to students at the University. He wrote books on religion and philosophy, and also brought out a biography of the great musician Bach, whom he loved and admired greatly. His astonishing creativity and versatility were admired by everyone.

In 1912, when he was 37 years of age, Albert married Helene – truly a soul-mate – who shared his spirit of selfless service. She was a great source of strength and support to him in his life of intense activity and creativity. She helped him in all his efforts.

Gifted with a brilliant intellect and a probing mind, Schweitzer also aspired to grow in the life of the Spirit. In his life of intense activity, there was also a sense of utter simplicity: he always travelled in a third-class carriage; he always carried his own luggage. He was a firm believer in the culture of manual labour.

When Albert saw the way blacks were being treated, and read about conditions in Africa, his conscience was stirred. His life took a new turn. He felt that Jesus was calling him to a life of service and dedication. He longed to do something for the African people – to share their burden, to help them, to make their life better in any way that was possible.

"I have always held firmly to the thought that each one of us can do a little to bring some portion of misery to an end," he said. And putting his belief into practice, Albert surprised his friends and family considerably by going back to college for a third time – at the age of 38. This time he acquired a fourth doctorate to become a real and proper doctor – a doctor of medicine. Not to be left out of his efforts, his wife took up training as a nurse, so that she could assist him in all his endeavours.

More than one University offered Dr. Schweitzer a chair – but he declined all their offers politely. He said, he had been born in this world not to make money, but to serve humanity, for the love of Jesus.

Even the people who had admired and respected him, failed to understand his aspirations. Some people called him quixotic, others called him eccentric. One man even remarked that too much learning had made Albert mad!

"They tried to dig fists into my heart," Albert said of them later. But all their digs and insults did not deter him from his purpose. He packed his bags for Africa, turning his back on a lucrative career, and a life of security and comfort.

He chose the backwoods of Lamberene to set up his mission of mercy. Lamberene was completely cut off from civilisation, and had no medical facilities to speak of. Undeterred, Dr. Schweitzer began to see his patients on an open plot of ground – a clearing adjacent to his dwelling.

It was not an easy life, administering even basic medical care in the African bush. Conditions were tough. It was exhausting to work under the scorching tropical sun. Every evening, there would be a thunderstorm, and all the medical equipment had to be taken indoors.

Dr. Schweitzer realised Lamberene desperately needed its own hospital – at least a small one to start with. Malaria, dysentery and leprosy were rampant among the natives.

Dr. Schweitzer did not belong to any church or voluntary organisation; he had chosen to work on his own – and that meant added responsibility. Unfortunately, many of the natives were not friendly, helpful or appreciative of his work.

Practically alone, Dr. Schweitzer carried on his work, helping and healing the people. In his spare time, he set about building a hospital. While the building was being constructed, he carried out surgical procedures in a windowless, leaking, poultry shelter!

It was a tough job constructing a hospital in the African backwoods. He would go to the forest and fell down the trees, chop the wood and carry logs on his shoulders to the site where the hospital was to be built. Toiling all by himself, log by log, he single-handedly raised the walls of his hospital building.

One day, while struggling with a heavy load of wood, which he could not manage, he spotted a black man lounging in the woods.

Politely, he requested the man, "Brother, can you give me a helping hand with this load?"

"Hey mister," came the haughty reply, "can't you see I'm an educated man?"

Dr. Schweitzer smiled and said, "I am happy, I am not educated!"

Many of Dr. Schweitzer's friends felt that he was throwing away his talents and his special training. Some of them even travelled to Africa to persuade him to come back to the land of his birth. "Why should you work here among these Africans?" they asked him. "What can a great and gifted man like you get out of all this painful struggle and hard labour?"

Schweitzer's reply was simple. "What does it matter where I live, provided I can do good work there? I appreciate your concern for me – but I have made up my mind to stay here and look after my African brothers and sisters."

The obstacles and challenges he faced were numerous. He had to contend with poisonous insects, wild animals, a difficult tropical climate and unknown infections; the natives were not easy to treat, for their faith was in black magic and witchcraft; and they were not really appreciative of the efforts of their benefactor. But Dr. Schweitzer did not give up his efforts.

After a few years, he went back to Europe for a brief period, to raise funds for his work. He gave organ recitals and delivered public lectures for fund-raising purposes. Huge crowds gathered to see him and hear him, and he was able to raise as much money as he needed to complete his hospital construction.

When he returned to Lamberene, the half-completed hospital had been overrun by the ever-spreading jungle. Grass and brushwood had grown over the walls and a thick growth covered the building.

Dr. Schweitzer had to begin all over again – but he never gave up his efforts, never gave in to despair. He was a man with a mission – and a man with great determination.

Over the years, he won the respect, affection and admiration of the natives. The rest of the world was not far behind in recognising and appreciating his spirit of selfless service. Honours and awards were heaped upon him. But he turned away from all public adulation, choosing to carry on with his mission of healing.

Dr. Schweitzer's compassion also extended to animals. He protested, again and again, against the cruel treatment men meted out to animals. "Let no one shirk the burden of his responsibility to animals," he said. "Think of the cries of the animals who are stuffed into railway trucks and thirst for water! Think of the pain we inflict on them in our cruel slaughter-houses! We are all guilty, and must bear the blame!"

In 1945, a British Newspaper wrote in commemoration of his 70th birthday: "If sainthood consists in making a virtuous life attractive, Albert Schweitzer is a saint of our century."

Dr. Schweitzer was awarded the Nobel Peace Prize in 1952. On his 80th birthday in 1955, he was awarded the Order of Merit, one of the highest distinctions of Great Britain. With all the funds he earned from his own royalties and personal appearances, fees and donations received from all over the world, he expanded his Hospital in Africa, which, by the early 1960's could take care of over 500 in-patients. The Nobel Prize money was used to set up a special leprosy center at Lamberene.

He worked in Lamberene till the last day of his life, and was buried near the hospital which he had built with so much love and care.

Let us pay homage to this great soul – acclaimed preacher, concert organist, internationally renowned scholar and an intellectual genius, who devoted his life to serve those less fortunate than himself!

Let us remember with love and admiration, this multi-faceted personality who was one of the most loved and respected men of our times!

Sayings of Albert Schweitzer

"By having a reverence for life, we enter into a spiritual relation with the world. By practising reverence for life we become good, deep, and alive."

* * * * *

"Compassion, in which all ethics must take root, can only attain its full breadth and depth, if it embraces all living creatures and does not limit itself to mankind."

* * * * *

"Constant kindness can accomplish much. As the sun makes ice melt, kindness causes misunderstanding, mistrust, and hostility to evaporate."

* * * * *

"Do something for somebody everyday for which you do not get paid."

* * * * *

"Example is not the main thing in influencing others. It is the only thing."

* * * * *

"Never say, there is nothing beautiful in the world anymore. There is always something to make you wonder in the shape of a tree, the trembling of a leaf."

* * * * *

"Revenge... is like a rolling stone, which, when a man hath forced up a hill, will return upon him with a greater violence, and break those bones whose sinews gave it motion."

* * * * *

"The purpose of human life is to serve, and to show compassion and the will to help others."

* * * * *

"The tragedy of life is what dies inside a man while he lives."

* * * * *

"We are all so much together, but we are all dying of loneliness."

Some Books by Albert Schweitzer

- *Out of My Life and Thought*
- *Quest of the Historical Jesus*
- *Reverence for Life*
- *Philosophy of Civilization*
- *Memoirs of Childhood and Youth*
- *Mysticism of Paul the Apostle*
- *The Light Within Us*
- *Mystery of the Kingdom of God: The Secret of Jesus' Messiahship and Passion*
- *The Animal World of Albert Schweitzer*
- *Psychiatric Study of Jesus*
- *Animals, Nature and Albert Schweitzer*
- *Peace or Atomic War?*
- *Pilgrimage to Humanity*

Some Books on Albert Schweitzer

- *Albert Schweitzer: A Biography* (The Albert Schweitzer Library) – by James Brabazon
- *Albert Schweitzer: Essential Writings* (Modern Spiritual Masters) – by James Brabazon
- *Albert Schweitzer's Mission: Healing and Peace* – by Norman Cousins
- *Albert Schweitzer* (Gateway Biographies) – by Harold Robles
- *My Days with Albert Schweitzer* – by Frederick Franck
- *All Men are Brothers: A Portrait of Albert Schweitzer* – by Charlie May Simon
- *Reverence for Life: The Ethics of Albert Schweitzer for the Twenty-First Century* – by Marvin Meyer (Editor), Kurt Bergel (Editor)
- *Schweitzer: A Biography* – by George Marshall

Sadhvi Vasuki

Sadhvi Vasuki was a pious and virtuous woman, who embodied the spirit of true Indian womanhood. An exemplary wife, she was a living example of the ideal *pativrata,* who demonstrated how married life could be turned into the way of salvation and liberation. The blessed consort of the great poet-saint Thiruvaluvar, Vasuki became his ideal soul-mate, and an inspiring role model for all married women.

Sadhvi Vasuki

There was a time when, in Chennai, there was in every home a scripture which is revered as the fifth Veda. We all are familiar with the four Vedas: The *Rig Veda,* The *Yajur Veda,* The *Atharva Veda* and The *Sama Veda.* The teachings of the fifth Veda are simple and practical and can be practised in one's daily life. It is a scripture of great practical value. It is called Thirukural, because it was written by a *bhakta* of the Lord, named Thiruvaluvar.

Thiruvaluvar was a great soul, a saint, a man of wisdom. Hundreds of thousands of people in South India worship this saint and read and recite from his sacred text even today.

Thiruvaluvar, like Sant Kabir, was a weaver. He earned his livelihood by weaving cloth. He was an honest man and his heart ever aspired to the True, the Good, the Beautiful, the Pure and the Perfect – *Satyam, Shivam, Sundaram, Pavitram, Purnam.* He subjected himself to several disciplines, and lived an austere life. One day, God's grace descended on him and his heart was enlightened. He uttered spiritual words of wisdom which are compiled in this sacred book called *Kural*.

In the *Kural* we are asked to be like the clouds which pour their rain upon all. The clouds do not discriminate between rich and poor, high and low. Neither do they refuse to shower their blessing on an apparently undeserving person. In the same way, we are asked to give the blessings of our hearts to all. Render love to all without distinction, the great poet urges us.

The sacred text contains many beautiful teachings. It is quite voluminous and serves to guide people who live the life of householders. Thiruvaluvar urged that, unlike many other saints, he did not believe that a *sanyasi*'s life was superior to that of a family man. He believed that the life of a *grahastha* was, in fact, superior to that of a *sanyasi*. For, he who fulfills all his duties as a family man, is indeed, blessed. Such a man, in fact, attains God faster and with much more ease than those who practise *sanyasa*.

In a similar vein, Sri Ramakrishna Paramahansa has taught that it is easier for a family man to attain to God. He compares the *grahastha* to the warrior who battles from within the walls of a fort. Such a warrior, by virtue of being within the fort, is safeguarded from all external attacks. On the other hand, a *sanyasi* who seeks to attain God, can be compared to a warrior who is battling in an open field, where he is exposed to attacks from all sides. Such a man is very often injured, as he is unable to protect himself. Thiruvaluvar has sung a number of poems in praise of the *grahastha ashrama*.

In one place, he says, "Fortunate is the husband who is blessed with a loyal, faithful and devoted wife." His book mentions several attributes and virtues of a faithful wife. Every true disciple would wish to imbibe the qualities of a loyal, faithful, devoted wife!

Thiruvaluvar's wife was an example to be emulated by everyone. Her name was Vasuki. She was one such devout and faithful wife. To her, her husband was the symbol of God. She firmly believed that her husband was her Master, her Lord. She considered serving him to be her sacred *dharma,* her sacred duty. She was indeed an ideal *grahasthi*.

Vasuki's name and fame as a true *pativrata* spread, far and wide. In those days, there was an ascetic named Konkan. Owing to his *tapasya,* he had acquired a number of supernatural powers. But, alas, the acquisition of those powers had made him arrogant. He had failed to subdue his ego.

Sadhu Vaswani often said, "If you have failed to annihilate your ego, then all your powers or *siddhis* are in vain. You will continue to remain in darkness!"

A person may recite the Name Divine constantly: he may live a life of intense austerity. But he will not be able to attain God until, and unless he learns to crush his ego, and become humble as ashes and dust. A person who fails to annihilate the ego, easily loses his temper over small and petty things. Anger, according to the teaching of the Gita, is a gateway to hell. If a person wishes to progress on the spiritual path, he must first learn to annihilate the ego.

Once Sri Ramakrishna Paramahansa was asked, "Pray tell us, why, in spite of all that you have done, the *sadhanas* you have practised, the austere life that you have lived, the depth of meditation in which you have delved, you have not bothered to attain *siddhis*, supernatural powers?

Sri Ramakrishna Paramahansa answered, "What shall I do with *siddhis* and miraculous powers? I do not need them. All that I need is to be close to the Divine Mother! I need nothing besides. Mother, keep me away from the desire to posses supernatural powers, so-called *siddhis*, for once a man gets entangled in them, the ego raises its ugly head."

The *Siddha,* Konkan, had heard about the fame and greatness of Thiruvaluvar and his wife, Vasuki. In his mind, he felt unhappy, because even though he had acquired miraculous powers, he had not become as famous as Vasuki and Thiruvaluvar. People did not sing praises of him as they did of the saintly couple. Disturbed, he decided to find out the reason for their popularity. He was tortured by questions such as, "Who are these people? What kind of *siddhis* do they possess? Are they superior to my *siddhis*? Do they have far more *siddhis* than I possess?" The *tapasvi* was determined to seek answers to those questions and so he decided to leave Chennai. As in those days, there were no vehicles, he undertook the journey on foot.

As he proceeded to Chennai, he saw some birds in flight. One of the bird's droppings fell on his bald head. He soiled his hand as he wiped his head. This infuriated him. The *tapasvi* had failed to master his ego and was prone to lose his temper over trifles. The bird's simple act infuriated him and with blood-shot eyes, he stared at the bird. The intensity of his anger was so great that the poor bird was burnt to ashes instantly. The bird dropped down dead in front of the *tapasvi*. This sight pleased the *tapasvi*. He felt that the bird deserved to die, as it had committed the sin of soiling his head and hand.

He proceeded on his journey to Chennai. He kept asking for Saint Thiruvaluvar's house and finally managed to reach it. Standing outside the house, he asked for alms. In those days it was an accepted norm that an ascetic must be attended to without delay. It was commonly assumed that ascetics must be accorded priority and householders were expected to give up their chores and engage in welcoming and attending to the holy alms-seekers.

The *tapasvi* standing outside Vasuki's house expected to be treated like a royal guest. He had no doubts that Vasuki, on hearing him, would come rushing out of the house to greet and welcome him. However, the expected did *not* happen. Vasuki, despite hearing him, failed to appear at the door at once. The *tapasvi* kept calling and wondered why Vasuki turned a deaf ear to his calls. As time elapsed, the *tapasvi*'s anger started mounting. How dare this woman, this ordinary housewife, ignore him?

Now-a-days, very few people like to entertain guests. Today, there is a rush for making money. Everyone wants to make more and more money. No one is prepared to attend to guests. But there was a time, when in India, guests were honoured and, in fact, thought of as images of God. The word for guest in Hindi is *'atithi'*, which literally means 'one who announces himself without any previous intimation'. In those early days, despite the unpredictability about the arrival of guests, it was customary to welcome them and serve them with love.

The *tapasvi* kept calling, but to no avail. What was Vasuki doing? Why did she not rush to greet her guest? The reason was that she was busy serving meals to her husband. Devout and faithful wife that she was, Vasuki heard the *tapasvi* calling, but decided that it was her duty first to serve her husband and then answer the call of the guest. After her husband finished his meals, she appeared at the door to welcome the guest. But the *tapasvi* by now, was seething with anger. With blood-shot eyes he looked at Vasuki.

When Konkan glared at her in wrath, Vasuki smiled at the *tapasvi* and asked him gently, "Swamiji, do you consider me to be a bird that you are glaring at me with such angry eyes?"

Those words gave the shock of his life to the *tapasvi*. He could not understand how Vasuki, who was sitting in her house, knew about the incident that occurred in the forest, miles away from her abode. Swiftly, as an arrow in flight, his heart was changed. He was transformed. Bowing before Vasuki, he said, "Mother, I had heard a lot about your greatness, but I never could imagine the extent of your powers. Now I wish to stay at your house and learn some essentials of life. Pray, permit me to do so."

Saint Thiruvaluvar graciously permitted Konkan to stay at their house. Konkan's stay was, indeed, fulfilling as he learnt many lessons in spirituality. Once he saw Vasuki drawing water from the well in her back-yard. One end of the rope was tied to the pot. With the help of the rope Vasuki put the pot in the well and started drawing water out. Slowly, but steadily she kept tugging at the rope and pulling the pot out of the well. Suddenly, she heard her husband call out her name. Without wasting a fraction of a second, without considering that it would take just a few additional seconds to fully pull out the pot of water, Vasuki left the rope and rushed to her husband. Konkan narrates that what he witnessed subsequently, was nothing short of a miracle. Konkan says, "This is something that I witnessed with my own eyes. I noticed that the pot remained steady and motionless at the level at which Vasuki left it. It remained in that position until Vasuki returned and pulled it up."

I do not know what really happened at that place, but, I can narrate a similar incident from my own life. I have spent some part of my youth in villages. One day, I went to a village and even as I was drawing out water from the well with the help of a bucket, I heard a heart-wrenching voice cry out, "Is there somebody who can save me?" Hearing the voice, I left the rope and moved in the direction of the cry. When I returned, I found the bucket at the level I had left it at. There was, however, no miracle there. In reality, there was a big stone in which the rope had got entangled; due to which the bucket was stationed where I left it. But, what happened in Vasuki's case I do not know. Such instances can happen and do happen. Konkan, however clearly recalls that he saw all this with his own eyes.

Konkan also narrates another incident. In his words, "Saint Thiruvaluvar was having breakfast and, I had joined him. I noticed that the rice that was served was very cold. At that time, Saint Thiruvaluvar called out to Vasuki and said, "Vasuki, my dear, the rice is steaming hot. Would you kindly bring a fan to cool the rice?"

Vasuki knew that the rice was cold but she did *not* react and say to her husband, "The rice is already cold!" Instead, the devout and faithful wife that she was, Vasuki obeyed her husband and started fanning the rice. Konkan adds, "I saw with my own eyes that as Vasuki fanned the rice, steam started arising from the cold rice."

There is no higher form of discipline than implicit obedience. That person is fortunate who follows the path of obedience. Till we learn the virtue of obedience, we keep getting entangled in the cycle of birth and death. Till we learn to become obedient, we can never hope to become truly free. The way to salvation is to tread the path of obedience. This was the path which this great woman of God, Vasuki, chose to tread.

Time rolled on. Vasuki was nearing the end of her earthly journey. She was on her sick bed and her husband was by her side. He looked at her lovingly. He sensed that there were some questions lingering in the mind of his dear, devoted wife. He could see it in her eyes. So, he said to her gently, "It appears that you want to ask me something." Until then, Vasuki had never raised any questions.

Everyday when she served meals to her husband, he would request her to put some water in a small conch shell, and a small pin beside him. Everyday, Vasuki did as she was told. Years had passed by. But never once did her husband make use of the water that was put in the shell, or the pin that was placed along with it. Now, when Vasuki was lying on her death bed, and her husband gave her permission to ask what she would, she said, she would like to know the meaning of what she was asked to do, everyday.

In answer Thiruvaluvar said, "Dear one, I had asked you to do so because, I felt that while you served meals to me, perchance, you might drop a grain of rice or a bit of vegetable, then I would pick up the same with the pin, put it in the water for cleansing, and place it back on my plate for consumption. I did this because I did not want to waste even a single grain of food." The saint continued, "However, in all these years, you have served me with such love and care that never ever did you spill a single grain out of the plate. Consequently, I could never put to use the shell or the pin."

In contrast to this, we spill and waste so much food, when we eat! Even though so many people go hungry in our country, look at the amount of wastage that takes place in our homes! Perhaps, you have not known this, but I have seen with my own eyes people at late hours of the night – at 1 A.M. or 2 A.M. – looking into garbage bins in search of food, in the hope that they might be lucky to find something to eat. Such being the condition of our people, we have no right to waste even a single grain of food! We must stop being careless even in the case of left-overs – even vegetable skins and stems that are discarded carelessly can be used to feed goats and cows. Doing so will bring you rich blessings. No food should ever be wasted; besides food, we should also ensure that there is no wastage of our precious time. We should put to good use each breath that we inhale and exhale!

We waste so many of our precious breaths. Each breath, each second is so precious. Let us learn to exercise self-discipline, self-restraint. Sri Krishna in the *Bhagavad Gita* says to Arjuna: "O Arjuna, the path of *yoga* is the path of self-control; gather the treasure of *Atmic shakti*; gather the treasure of the Name Divine. Such is the way to salvation or *mukti*."

But, to return to the life of Vasuki. Soon thereafter, Vasuki dropped her physical body. But she continues to live in the hearts of millions of devoted women, to whom she has become a role model. Some of her rare qualities are captured in the *Kural*, as the essence of a true wife:

1) She always praises and honours her husband.

2) She respects and obeys his every word.

3) She goes to bed after her husband had fallen asleep; she rises before he awakens, so that she could serve him at all times.

4) She is the very picture of love, devotion, loyalty, faith and obedience.

Are not those the qualities of an ideal disciple as well?

If only we, too, followed the path of self-discipline and obedience, and learnt to collect the true treasure of the Spirit, we too, would be blessed!

Sahl Darvesh

Sahl Darvesh was a saint whose quest was to discover the true purpose of human life – and to fulfill the purpose for which God had created him. He was one of those rare souls who constantly communed with the Divine Spirit and became aware that God is all-pervasive; that God is watching us at all times, in all places. Sahl was God-intoxicated; God-filled. His faith and devotion drew many souls Godward. He gave up all he had, to pursue his faith, and the Lord blessed him and accepted his devotion.

Sahl Darvesh

The human birth is, in truth, a great gift from God. We are told that after a cycle of hundreds and thousands of mineral, vegetable and animal existances, we have obtained the human birth. Therefore, we should not fritter it away, but live to realise its true purpose.

About twelve centuries ago, a saint was born. His name was Sahl. He realised that God had given him the human birth for a specific purpose which he must discover and fulfill.

When he was a young boy, he repeatedly asked himself, "Why has God given me the human birth? People, alas, fritter away the precious human birth in amassing money and in pursuit of power, pleasure and pelf. But surely, this is not the purpose of the human birth." Thus, he would, again and again, pray: "O Lord, do bless me that I may fulfill the purpose for which the human birth has been given to me."

One day his disciples asked Sahl, "We wish to know about your childhood. Will you kindly tell us about the earliest memory you have as a child?"

Sahl's answer surprised many of his listeners. The earliest memory he recounted was when he was in his mother's womb. "I was clustered up and clamouring in the dark. I clearly remember that I pleaded with God to release me from my confinement in the mother's womb." Thus, even in the womb of his mother, Sahl was a unique child.

Another experience he shared with his disciples was of the time when he was barely three years old. He would stay awake at night and call out to God, whom he called Allah, with tears flowing freely down his cheeks. He also narrated how his uncle, would see Sahl sitting awake late into the night and would ask him to go back to sleep. Only to please him, Sahl would lie down for a while, pretending to be asleep; but actually he would wait for his uncle to go back to sleep, so that he could sit up again, and commune with God.

Another experience he recounted was of the time when he was fifteen years old. He heard an angelic voice that said to him, "Am I not your Master?" He immediately knelt down and acknowledged: "Yes, Lord, You are my Master. I am Your slave."

In every thought, action and word, Sahl remembered his Master and his only aspiration was that in each thought, word and deed, he should glorify Him. "His Mercy like a magnet pulls me Godwards," Sahl would exclaim.

When Sahl was seven, his uncle called him and said to him, "Sahl, I am passing on a prayer to you.

Repeat it, again and again, and delve into the depths of the meaning of this prayer." It was a prayer which all of us, irrespective of our religion, caste, or colour can repeat with fervour: It is a universal prayer. It can be easily remembered by anyone. The words of the prayer are: "God is with me, God is witnessing me! God is watching over me!"

Is this not the teaching of all the saints and sages of East and West? It was Bayazid, who said, "I went out in search of God. I went here and there. I looked for Him everywhere. Filled with disappointment, as I was sitting in silence one day, I heard a voice say, "He is with you, He is within you, then why go in search of Him outside of yourself?"

The disease of loneliness has spread, far and wide. Even while staying within a family or while working in an office, surrounded by colleagues, the feeling of isolation gnaws at our vitals. This disease is spreading everywhere, because we have cut ourselves off from God. The cure for this disease is to have faith in the teaching of the saints, that we are not alone, God is with us, wherever we go. There is not a nook, not a corner where He is not. Significant are the words of the great English poet Tennyson: "Closer is He to us than breathing, nearer than hands and feet." If we wish to contact God, all we are required to do is to close our eyes, shut out the world, call Him with deep longing of the heart – and here He is in front of us. How true are the words, "God is with us, God is witnessing us. God is watching over us."

Let me tell you of a father who lost his job. In spite of his best efforts, he was unable to find another one. Eventually all his savings were wiped out. He was horrified to think that in order to provide the bare necessities for his family, he would be forced to steal.

Everyday, this man used to pass by a bungalow, the doors and windows of which were always closed. "Perhaps, nobody stays in it," he thought to himself. "So let me go in and steal something from there."

He took his little son with him and said to him, "Stand outside and blow this whistle if you find anyone watching us."

The father had just climbed the wall and jumped over to the other side, when he heard the sound of the whistle. Immediately, he jumped back and returned to his son. He looked here and there but found no one on the street. "Son, why did you blow the whistle?" he asked the little boy.

The son replied, "Today, we were taught at school, that God is witnessing us all the time. So God is here, watching you. How can you steal?" If only we bear witness to this teaching of Sahl Darvesh – a teaching which is as simple as it is great – our lives would indeed become new!

>God is with me!
>
>God is watching me!
>
>God is watching over me!

There were some who grew jealous of Sahl's popularity. One day, Sahl asked the people to pray to

God: "O Lord, forgive my faults and also pardon my good deeds." A *dervish* who lived in the town and heard of this, started telling the people that what Sahl taught was heresy. He disuaded the people from going to Sahl. Sahl learnt of it but did not utter a single word in self-defence. The mark of a true holy man of God is that he will never say anything in self-defence.

What Sahl Darvesh meant by his prayer was that when a good deed is done, we think that *we* have done it; this thought is like adding a drop of poison to a cup of milk: the entire milk is poisoned. Actually, by ourselves, we can do nothing. We are like bulbs: without the electric current we can do nothing. If we spread light, the credit must go to the electric current. It is God's *shakti* that is doing all the work: therefore, we should beg forgiveness for thinking that good deeds are being done by us. God's power is working in and through all of us. We can only do something good when God Wills it. Therefore, let us glorify God!

As his pilgrimage upon earth drew to a close, Sahl Darvesh said to his disciples, "The time has come for me to leave this town." He took a piece of paper and tore it to pieces. On each piece of paper he wrote down each of the possessions belonging to him. He called everyone and said, "I will throw these bits of paper in the breeze. Whoever picks up a piece, will receive the gift which is mentioned on it." Thus, he gave away all his possessions. After that he was never seen again. Nobody knows where he disappeared and when and where he passed away!

Darvesh Sahl is gone: but his prayer remains with us. It is a powerful prayer with tremendous *shakti* that can transform our daily life:

>God is with me!
>God is watching me!
>God is watching over me!

Sant Avvaiyar

Avvaiyar is a woman saint beloved of all Tamil people, who begin their education by reciting her immortal lines. Indeed, she is beloved of all seekers, for her life is a remarkable blend of wisdom and piety, pragmatism and faith, sound common sense and deep devotion. As a young girl, she turned her back on the life of material pleasures and the senses, and dedicated her life to the quest of truth and the uplift of suffering humanity. Her life was blessed by the Lord, and she was a blessing to countless souls, whose lives she touched.

Sant Avvaiyar

Avvaiyar was a holy woman who was known as the "Bride of God". She was born in South India in the ninth century. She was orphaned at a young age and was brought up by her foster parents. As her fasterfather was a poet, the little girl grew up in the soulful environs of the poet's house. Since childhood, she had an affinity for poetry. Her heart was filled with the spirit of compassion. Whenever she would come across a poor, starving man, she would take something from the house, to offer it to him.

She was fond of solitude. Often she would go to a quiet corner under the shade of a tree, or on the banks of a river, and sit by herself. She would ponder on the purpose of life, the meaning behind our human existence. She would meditate deeply on the thought: "People come to this earth and then depart. No one lives here forever. Is it not strange that, the time spent on earth, is spent in shouts and shows, but when the 'Call' comes, everything becomes silent again!"

One day, when the Call comes to us, we too, will have to leave everything behind – our wealth, our homes, our friends – all, all will be left behind! So, this little girl asked herself, "This life has surely been given to us for some special purpose. What is that purpose?"

She possessed a sharp intellect and as a child she was also a voracious reader. She would read about the lives of great ones, of saints and sages and would try to translate the teachings into deeds of daily living. She would say to herself, "I will achieve nothing merely by reading. I must put the teachings into practice."

Yes, only that which we actually imbibe in our daily lives is of real use to us. Else all other words and teachings only become a burden on us. Therefore, let us take up just *one* ideal or principle, and make it an inseparable part of our life. If we assimilate even one ideal and bear witness to it in our daily life, our sojourn on earth will be truly blessed!

Gradually, through long hours of study and contemplation, Avvaiyar began to enrich her inner life. She dived into the depths within herself and realised that the gift of the human birth is bestowed on us so that we may know our true Self, our Divine identity.

Avvaiyar was a very pretty woman. Her face was beautiful to behold. She had long silky hair. As she grew in years, she also grew in inner beauty and knowledge and developed the qualities of detachment and sacrifice. Her beauty captivated the minds and hearts of many who looked at her.

In those days, in India, there were many small kingdoms. News about Avvaiyar's beauty reached the ears of many kings. They sought her hand in marriage.

A prince of a neighbouring kingdom personally came to plead with her father to accept him as his son-in-law. The father thought to himself: "Such a great prince has personally come forward to ask for my daughter's hand in marriage. But, Avvaiyar is not interested in marriage. She has decided to dedicate her life to spiritual pursuits and service of the poor. The prince, if he so desired, could have commanded me to go to him, and I would have gone to him at once. But, he himself has come to me. How can I turn down his request?"

The father made his decision. He refused to listen to Avvaiyar and insisted that she accepted the proposal. What could Avvaiyar do? She felt helpless. Neither her father, nor her mother were prepared to listen to her. Besides them, there was no one else to whom she could turn for help and guidance.

Avvaiyar was confused. Near her house was a Vigneshwar Temple. Avvaiyar went to the temple and shed tears. She prayed to the Lord, "I had vowed that my life would be an offering at Your Feet, in service of the poor and needy. Now You must guide me, and tell me what I should do! My parents are forcing me to get married. I do not wish to do so. Why do these kings and princes desire to marry me? They are only enamoured of my external beauty and youth. No one is aware or concerned about what is *within me*. O Lord, take away my youth and beauty, so that I may be free to follow my aspirations. I wish to dedicate my life to You and You alone!"

A miracle came to pass. Overnight, Lord Ganesha turned the young maiden into an old, grey-haired woman. When she returned home, her parents could not recognise her. As for her princely suitors, they fled from her in consternation!

She willingly made such a great sacrifice of her youth and beauty. But for her it was not a sacrifice, for it brought her the freedom she intensely prayed for.

There had been a time when poems were sung of her beauty, but now it was the fame of her knowledge and wisdom and her profound social consciousness that spread far and wide. Kings invited her to come to their palaces. They would discuss their problems with her and take her advice on the affairs of their kingdoms. They would then follow her advice in letter and spirit. This would bring them tremendous benefit. Due to this, many kings invited her to live in their palace. But Avvaiyar always told them, "The pomp and splendour of the palace is not for me. I am a friend and companion of the poor. I belong to those who suffer and are in need."

She led a very simple life. The poor would call out to her, '*Amma, Amma*'. People referred to her as '*Jagat Amma*' or 'Universal Mother'.

To those who came to her she would say, "All that God has given you is a *loan* to be passed on to those whose need is greater than yours." Many people today, think that they should accumulate sufficient wealth first, become rich, save some money and then from those savings give away a little in charity. But Avvaiyar would say, "If you do this, you will never be able to give."

To elucidate this, she gave a beautiful example. She said, "If you are standing on the sea-shore and say, that you will take bath in the waters of the ocean only when the waves have subsided, days will roll into months and months into years and you will still be standing on the shore; because the waves in the ocean will never be stilled. Similarly, if you want to give in charity, begin *today!* Don't wait till you are wealthy enough and have saved plenty of money."

Yes, my friends, whatever we possess, does not belong to us. If it were really ours, we would be able to carry it with ourselves as we enter the Great Beyond after death. As this is not possible, let us realise that whatever we have, has been given to us so that we can share it with those in need.

Avvaiyar offered her entire life in service of the surrounding world. She started a *satsang*, so that she could help those in sorrow and suffering, to come closer to God. Those who were destitute and in need of help, started coming to her *satsangs* in large numbers.

She composed numerous songs and verses, which are still recited, by every child who learns Tamil.

One day, she was extremely hungry. This happened ever so often. Living amidst the poor, there were days when she herself would not get anything to eat. Often, she would go without food for two or three days. This did not perturb her. She was never worried or concerned about her body. She would say, "This body is an instrument of God. It is His responsibility to maintain it and care for it. If He sends me food to eat, I will feed my body. If He does not send any food, I will gladly fast for His sake."

Once, she had been constrained to fast for some days, and she looked weak and feeble. A man who saw her, said to her, "It appears that you are very hungry. Please come with me to my house. I will give you some food to eat." He took her to his home. But on reaching there he requested her to wait outside in the courtyard, for he was afraid of his wife, who was quarrelsome by nature.

The man was then in a quandary: how could he muster enough courage to ask his wife to give some food for the *Sadhvi?* His wife was a shrew, and fear made him feel helpless. But, somehow, he mustered courage, entered the house and tried to bring his wife into a good mood by talking sweetly to her. He took a comb and gently combed her hair. After giving her a lot of attention, he told her, "I have a guest with me. She looked really hungry. I would like to give her some food." On hearing those words from her husband, the wife exploded with rage. Fire emanated from her lips in the form of offensive words.

As she was talking in a sharp and loud voice, her words reached the ears of Avvaiyar. She smiled and called the man outside, saying, "Brother, please do not worry. I am going back. Do not give any trouble to your wife. But before I go, I wish to tell you something and that is this: marriage is pleasant — but only when one's wife is understanding and affectionate. If she isn't, then marriage is a veritable hell, and the only recourse, the only remedy to it, is *sanyasa*." To this day, people repeat her words in Tamil: "If you do not have an affectionate and understanding wife, just take up *sanyasa*, without a word to anyone."

There have been many such incidents in Avvaiyar's life. One teaching which she always emphasised was, "Speak sweetly, be careful and see that not one harsh word escapes your lips. There is tremendous strength in sweetness." She offered the following example: A mountain stands tall with such strength and stability, that it would be quite difficult to try and break it down. But a tender plant tears apart that surface of the firm mountain when its roots break through its soil. Hence, become soft, become sweet and tender.

Confucius was a great sage of China. When the last moments of his life drew close, a group of devotees sat around his death-bed. Confucius called one of them and, opening his mouth, said to him, "Tell me, what is there in my mouth?"

The devotee looked into the Master's mouth and said, "Master, there is only the tongue in your mouth and not even a single tooth."

Then said Confucius – and this was, perhaps, his last message: "My tongue is older than my teeth. I was born with the tongue: the teeth appeared later. Teeth appear to be strong, they are so hard. But, one by one, the strong teeth fall off. The tongue, which is so soft, continues to be in a perfect condition till the end. Therefore, always remember to be of a soft, tender temperament. If you are soft and sweet, you will survive till the end. Softness is the secret of lastingness."

Homage to Saint Avvaiyar who propagated through precept and example the ideals of simplicity, service and sweetness of temper.

Sayings of Sant Avvaiyar

"Do something good for others, daily."

* * * * *

"Don't advertise your wealth."

* * * * *

"Don't be dependent on others."

* * * * *

"Start eating, only after you offer food to others."

* * * * *

"Get along with everyone."

* * * * *

"Don't give up reading good books."

* * * * *

"Don't speak ill of others."

* * * * *

"Always speak decently and kindly."

* * * * *

"Understand your friends before you get close to them."

* * * * *

"Take care of your parents."

* * * * *

"Don't earn your living by deceiving others."

* * * * *

"Don't utter cruel words."

* * * * *

"Resolve to protect those who need protection."

* * * * *

"Lead a useful and productive life."

* * * * *

"Try to learn by asking questions."

* * * * *

"Share your skills with others."

Book by Sant Avvaiyar

- Athichoodi

Some Books on Sant Avvaiyar

- *Avvaiyar – Andru Mudal Indru Varai*: (Avvaiyar– From Then Until Now) – by Dr. Thayammal Aravanan
- *Avvaiyar Valvum Vakkum* (Avvaiyar – Her Life and Her Works) – by Ti Muttu-Kannappan
- *The Yoga of Siddha Avvai* – by S. N. Kandaswamy

Sadhu Hiranand

Sadhu Hiranand was an ideal teacher, a selfless servant of suffering humanity, a helper and healer, who was truly an instrument of God in a world of pain and illness. His life bore witness to the ideals of sympathy, service and sacrifice. A servant of truth, a votary of compassion, he created a new environment of idealism and high values, wherever he worked. In him, people saw a rare blend of greatness and goodness. He inspired a whole generation of youngsters with his living example.

Sadhu Hiranand

A holy man appeared in Sind in the 19th century. He was known as Sadhu Hiranand. Fragrant was his life as incense which is burnt at the Lord's holy feet. His life was a musical melody of silent service to those in suffering and pain.

As a college student, he kept a "journal", in which he noted down some of his thoughts and aspirations. On one page, in the "journal", we read the following soliloquy:

> What do you mean to do in life?
> To win praise and applause?
> No! To sacrifice.
> But how?
> I do not know yet!

This, perhaps, was the deepest aspiration of his heart — to be a faithful child of God. Sadhu Hiranand was born in Hyderabad-Sind on March 23, 1863. He did his daily work, offering it all at the Lotus Feet of the Lord. He had no thought of personal gain or reward, of name or fame or earthly greatness. He edited two weeklies but loved to be in the background. He was the Head master of a big school but drew not a paisa by way of salary. He did a lot of work which brought about reform in society, but he shunned the glare of publicity and prominence. He learnt Homeopathy and became a doctor in order that, in the words of Dr. Albert Schweitzer, he might be able "to serve without having to talk." Today, there is noise in our service: there are shouts and shows. Sadhu Hiranand revealed what it was to serve silently. Of him, it has been truly said that he was a "humble soul," humble and upright, pure and holy.

Sadhu Hiranand believed in the transforming power of education. He started in Hyderabad-Sind a School – The Academy – which, in due course, became the biggest School in the Bombay Presidency. It was a school offering a unique type of education. For, Sadhu Hiranand believed, that the purpose of a school was not to train students to secure jobs, amass money and live comfortable lives. A school must train its students to live not for self alone, but also for others.

In Hiranand's School studied Gurudeva Sadhu Vaswani. Sadhu Vaswani always spoke of Sadhu Hiranand as an "ideal teacher" and, in earlier days, when Sadhu Vaswani was a student in his school, Sadhu Hiranand spoke of Child Vaswani as a "model pupil". Sadhu Hiranand would take young Sadhu Vaswani from class to class and tell the students: "Here is an ideal student!"

To his students Sadhu Hiranand taught that life must be simple. The simple way was Hiranand's way. He was simple in dress and diet. He possessed that inner simplicity which is a rare virtue. Out of simplicity grows concentration. Hiranand was a graduate of Calcutta University. His special subjects were philosophy and literature.

In his teaching, Sadhu Hiranand laid emphasis on the quality of purity. He said to the students: "See that your eyes are pure. They must never look at anyone with lust. Refrain from drinking liquor and meat-eating. And in every woman, in every girl, in every human being, try to behold the Beauty of God!" Hiranand's own heart was clean, his eyes were pure and his mind was incorruptible. Therefore, his body, his entire being, was radiant with light.

Sadhu Hiranand gave the service of love to all. He would often say, "ye who belong to different religions and races, classes and communities – Ye all are one!"

In Sadhu Hiranand's Academy, were Hindu and Muslim students. There was one common tap from which all children had to drink water. Feeling thirsty, a Hindu student went to the tap to have a drink of water. He found a Muslim student drinking out of the tap. Those were the days of touch-me-notism and the Hindu student hesitated to drink water from the tap out of which a Muslim had just taken a drink.

Sadhu Hiranand happened to pass by and observed the hesitation on the part of the Hindu student. He wanted to teach this boy the great truth of the Unity of all religions.

To the Hindu student he said with a gentle chuckle, "Drink out of the tap and quench your thirst. Then wash off the pollution by cleaning your mouth with soap and water."

A cholera epidemic broke out in Hyderabad, spreading throughout the town, causing widespread suffering and death. Sadhu Hiranand moved as an angel of mercy from house to house, giving relief to the sick. He gave Homoeopathic medicines free: he charged no visiting fees. And he took no precautions for his own health. God gave him the gift of healing; and it is said, that 99% of those who took his sweet, tiny pills, were saved from the jaws of death.

One night, he returned home, tired after the day's work. He felt hungry and asked for food. And just as he was about to take the first morsel, a knock was heard on the door.

"Who is there?" asked Hiranand.

"We need you urgently, to attend to our cholera-stricken patient," the stranger replied.

He returned the morsel to the plate, got up, took his medicine-chest and, without a minute's delay, went out to attend to the ailing person.

His elder brother, Sadhu Navalrai, said to him, "You are tired and you are hungry. Why not ask the man to wait for a few minutes until you have taken your food?"

Sadhu Hiranand quietly replied, "Who knows, if I wait for a few minutes, it may be too late!"

He never thought of his own comfort: he always thought of giving relief to others.

Sadhu Hiranand's life was one of unceasing service. In his heart was a deep longing for silence, the deep stillness of the soul. Again and again, he would retire to a quiet corner and, sitting in silence, far from the madding crowds, he would commune with God.

Sadhu Hiranand was a giver. He gave and gave and ever gave. He gave of his time and talents, his energy and knowledge, his very life to those in need. He gave as the rain, which gives itself to all. If he had two coats, he gave one to him who had none. And he would not eat his food without first sharing it with a hungry man or woman.

Brief was his life on earth. But in the few years he worked, he achieved so much. Nothing was difficult for him. He worked, he laboured, he toiled: he served tirelessly like one who had a race to run against time! He did more for God and man in a month than many of us can do in a life-time!

He passed away in far-off Patna, in 1893, at the young age of 30. It is said that they whom the gods love, die young! He nursed his dear daughter until he caught from her the fatal fever which brought his brief, beautiful life to a sudden end. "I am not afraid of death!" he said, "To die is to go on a pilgrimage." As a pilgrim, he lived his brief span of life on earth and as a pilgrim he moved out of it. Blessed be his memory!

I bow down to him and exclaim: "The life of Sadhu Hiranand was a garden in which a thousand roses bloomed and a hundred nightingales sang their songs. The roses have withered, but their fragrance remains! The nightingales are no more: but their song continues to thrill many-a-heart with the message: Life and all the bounties of life are given us to be spent in service of the surrounding world!"

Some Books on Sadhu Hiranand

- *Sadhu Hiranand: (the soul of modern Sind)* – by C.T. Valecha
- *Sadhu Hiranand and the city of God* (Sangha series) – by Jamini Kanta Koar
- *Sadhu Hiranand: The man and his mission* – by Gobind Malhi

Sister Nivedita

India has reason to feel eternally grateful to some westerners who, when the country was passing through a period of darkness and despair, gave hope and strength to the people. One of them was **Sister Nivedita**, who dedicated the best years of her life to the service of India and her teeming millions. Inspired by Swami Vivekananda's teachings, she dedicated her life to spreading his message. She was a woman of faith and courage, of vision and wisdom. And she urged, if every Indian could spend ten minutes every evening and remind himself that we all who belong to different races and religions, castes and communities, are children of *Bharat Mata*, India could be one of the greatest nations of the world.

Sister Nivedita

In 1893, the World-Parliament of Religions was inaugurated in Chicago, U.S.A. Swami Vivekananda had gone to participate in the Parliament, as India's representative. He had no money with him: but he had the greatest treasure – faith in God and the Guru. He went to the Parliament of Religions and sat quietly in a corner, a picture of humility. When it was his turn to speak, he took the American public by storm! His words left a deep impact on people's hearts and they were mesmerised. They desired to hear him, again and again.

He continued to stay on in the States after the Parliament was over. He was invited to speak at many more places, in different parts of the United States. He also received invitations from other countries. In 1895, he went to England. He spoke to spiritual aspirants in many places there. Although the meetings were attended by small groups of people, within their hearts was thirst for God, and reverence for the ancient Indian culture. They were, indeed, the chosen few, the privileged few!

According to one account, at one such meeting, there were only about 15 to 17 people present. Among them was a very special woman. Her name was Miss Margaret Noble. Today, she is known as Sister Nivedita.

On the very first occasion when Margaret Noble came to listen to Swami Vivekananda's lecture, she watched him intently and listened to his speech attentively. When the lecture was over, some of the people asked her how she had liked Swamiji's lecture. In response, she casually remarked, "It was okay. Swamiji did not mention anything new or special in his lecture." But after she returned home she began to ask herself, "Why did I speak those words? Swamiji had in fact mentioned many new things. Why did I say that nothing new or special was said by him?"

After that, every time that Swami Vivekananda gave a lecture, Margaret would make sure she attended it. She started listening to him very attentively. Gradually, Swami Vivekananda's teachings penetrated her heart and, as a result, she developed a deep affection for India's ancient culture and heritage.

Swami Vivekananda returned to America after his eight-month trip to England. A year later, he came once again to England. Whenever Swami Vivekananda gave a lecture, Margaret Noble was sure to be there. One day, Swami Vivekananda said to her, "India has need of women like you. At this time, we need people who will help the women-folk of India and try to uplift them. We need to educate them." When Margaret Noble heard those words, she said, "I am ready!"

In January 1898, she came to Calcutta, and told Swami Vivekananda, "Swamiji, I feel this is the beginning of a new life for me. It is a new phase of my life. So, please bestow on me a new name." Vivekananda agreed. In the presence of many *swamis* who got together at the Belur Math, the sacred *havan* fire was lit and Swami Vivekananda gave her the name by which she is known all over the world today – Sister Nivedita. She was initiated and made a *brahmacharini*. The meaning of the word "Nivedita" is, "one who has offered herself completely, wholly, to God – the dedicated one". She lived up to her name, in every sense of that term, till the very last breath of her life.

Sister Nivedita worked extremely hard. To start with, she opened a school for girls, as she felt that it was only through education that the country could be transformed and made new.

Then, all of a sudden, an epidemic of plague struck Calcutta. People panicked. When anyone was struck by plague, even their near and dear ones abandoned them and left the house. At such a time, this English woman went from house to house and offered her services. She would literally knock at their door and ask, "Is there any service required, please let me know. I am ready to serve you." She pleaded with the people, "If you want to stop the spread of plague, then keep the city clean. Keep your homes clean."

One day, she saw some filth in the street. This English woman, who had a special place in her heart for India and the Indians, took up a broom and started sweeping the streets. When people learnt of this, they came running and said to her, "This work is not for you to do: We are going to do it ourselves." Groups of young men were formed in different parts of the city, who started cleaning the streets of Calcutta. This English lady, by sweeping the streets herself, had set an example to be emulated.

Swami Vivekananda decided to visit the West for the second time. Sister Nivedita accompanied Swamiji and collected funds for her School in Calcutta. Both Guru and disciple left together. Sister Nivedita had tremendous devotion for her Guru, though in one of her books she has written, "Very often, I could not understand my Guru's ideas. I would argue with him on many topics. Our arguments would last for several hours. But, even then, I would not agree with him. Then once, while I was sitting in silence, I asked myself, "Why do I argue with my Guru thus?" From within me I got the answer, "It's because of the ego." Indeed, it is the ego that needs to be annihilated. For, if there is one thing that stands between the disciple and the Guru, it is the ego.

The Guru and the disciple travelled abroad. It is said, "When you embark on a journey in the company of your Guru, the journey becomes a sacred pilgrimage." This journey was veritably a pilgrimage for Sister Nivedita. Every morning, Swami Vivekananda would come and sit on the deck of the ocean-liner on which both were travelling. Sister Nivedita would sit at his feet and absorb the teachings of Swami

Vivekananada. She noted down everything that Swamiji told her. It is said, that if Sister Nivedita had not jotted down those notes, then many of Swamiji's teachings would have been lost to us.

On Wednesday, July 2, 1902, Sister Nivedita came from Calcutta to Belur Math to meet Swami Vivekananda. It was the sacred *Ekadashi* day. Swamiji greeted her with great love and affection. Even though he was fasting, he wanted a feast to be prepared for her. Vegetable curries and rice and fruits and curdled milk were all brought for Sister Nivedita. Inspite of Sister Nivedita's reluctance to eat, Swamiji served her with his own hands. After eating, when Sister Nivedita wished to wash her hands, Swamiji himself brought the jug of water for her and a napkin, saying, "I will pour the water for you." Then he gave her a napkin to wipe her hands. Sister Nivedita immediately remarked, "Swamiji, you are doing what I should be doing. What is the reason?" The answer Swami Vivekananda gave, startled Sister Nivedita. "Did not Jesus also wash the feet of his disciples?" Sister Nivedita recalled, "At that time it occurred to me to say to Swamiji, but Jesus did that when his final moment was near. But I preferred to be silent."

As Swami Vivekananda lived in Belur and Sister Nivedita in Calcutta, two days later, on Friday, he sent a message mentioning that he was absolutely fine. But on Saturday morning, Sister Nivedita got the news that Swami Vivekananda had suddenly passed away the previous night. The news came to her as a rude shock: she felt deeply stunned. For a few moments she was speechless. She rushed to Belur. From morning till noon, she sat near the Guru's body, all the while fanning his lifeless form. After Swamiji's body had been cremated, turning to the people present there, Sister Nivedita said, "Do not think that our Guru has left us and gone away. Our Guru is always with us! He is telling us that we should serve Mother India with even more dedication and determination."

Sister Nivedita plunged herself in the service of India. She said, "India will be free only when Indians obtain a new type of education. There can be salvation only when India is united."

Sister Nivedita gave a number of lectures encouraging the youths to dedicate themselves to the service of India. The year 1904 saw Sister Nivedita and Rabindra Nath Tagore draw close to each other, in a bond of friendship. Both of them spoke from common platforms. Rabindra Nath Tagore was deeply impressed by the depth of Sister Nivedita's knowledge. Some of Rabindra Nath Tagore's patriotic songs were translated into English by Sister Nivedita.

Then came the devastating flood in East Bengal. Sister Nivedita rendered tremendous relief services. She sacrificed her personal comforts, caring little for her health. Soon thereafter, she fell ill.

While she lay ill, she was visited by the great scientist, Jagdish Chandra Bose, who requested her to take a few days off for rest and recuperation at Darjeeling.

"Rest?" Sister Nivedita replied with a smile, "Where is the time for rest? There is so much still to be done!" Her health continued to deteriorate.

In 1911, she left for Darjeeling, bidding farewell to each one individually before her departure. At that time, Ma Sharadhamani had gone to her village and in her place there was Jogan Ma. Sister Nivedita said to her, "Ma, I feel as though I am bidding farewell to you for the last time." To this Jogan Ma replied, "Your age is not far advanced. You are still young. Why are you talking in this manner? Do not even let such thoughts enter your mind."

Soon after reaching Darjeeling, Sister Nivedita was afflicted by severe dysentery. At 7 a.m. on October 13, she breathed her last and passed on to become one with her Guru.

Sister Nivedita! There is a fragrance in her name. It is the fragrance of a dedicated life. What is there that Sister Nivedita did not do for India and her people? For fourteen years, she served tirelessly. Today, we have forgotten her. But a new age will dawn, when Indians will remember, with gratitude, all those who served the Motherland selflessly. Then, indeed, Sister Nivedita's name will surely be written in letters of gold.

Homage to her!

Sayings of Sister Nivedita

"Like the large pulsation, made up of innumerable small pulses fused in one, so is every great and clear act of the mind, or intuition of the soul made up of the results of countless efforts, countless experiences of the past. An irresistible conjecture is often unremembered knowledge."

* * * * *

"As long as ego remains, so long the wheel revolves. Lose ego in love. Lose love in sacrifice for others. So the Beloved becomes the Divine, and the lover forgets self."

* * * * *

"I believe that India is one, indissoluble, indivisible."
"National unity is built on the common home, the common interest and common love."

* * * * *

"Can we not cultivate in our children and ourselves a vast compassion? This compassion will make us eager to know the sorrows of all men, the griefs of our land and the dangers to which, in these modern days, the religion is exposed; and this growing knowledge will produce strong works, working for work's sake, ready to die, if only they may serve their country and fellow-men."

Some Books by Sister Nivedita

- An Indian Study of Love and Death
- Cradle Tales on Hinduism
- Kali, the Mother
- Studies from an Eastern Home
- The Web of Indian Life
- The Master as I saw Him
- Footfalls of Indian history
- Studies From An Eastern Home
- Notes of Some Wanderings With Swami Vivekananda
- Hints On National Education In India
- Siva and Buddha
- Civic & National Ideals
- Swamiji and His Message
- The Complete Works of Sister Nivedita – by Margaret Elizabeth Noble

Some Books on Sister Nivedita

- Sister Nivedita: Pioneer in Missionary Work – by S. R. Bakshi
- The Dedicated: Biography of Sister Nivedita – by Lizelle Reymond
- Sister Nivedita in Search of Humanity: A study in social and political ideas – by Santana Mukherjee
- The Story of Sister Nivedita – by Atmaprana
- Sister Nivedita of Ramakrishna-Vivekananda – by Pravrajika Atmaprana
- My India, My People – Sister Nivedita – by Pravrajika Atmaprana
- Nivedita As I Saw Her – Translated by Probhati Mukherjee from the Bengali Nibeditake Jemon Dekhiyachhi by Saralabala Sarkar

Swami Rama Lingam

Swami Rama Lingam was one of the notable saints of South India to appear in the nineteenth century. An ardent exponent of Shiva *bhakti,* he arrived at great religious truths intuitively without relying on formal education. A man with great love and compassion for all living beings, he was also a firm advocate of *annadana* or feeding of the poor. A realised soul, he believed that eternal bliss was union with God – and true to his belief, attained *samadhi* through dematerialisation.

Swami Rama Lingam

Shri Rama Lingam Swami was born in a village near Chidambaram in South India.

Gurudev Sadhu Vaswani often said, "God dwells in the villages: the cities are homes of Satan." Little wonder, that so many of our saints sages and holy ones have taken birth in villages. The environment of the village is pure and holy. The villagers live in the love and fear of God. They speak the truth. They welcome guests and serve them with respect and love. They are free from the allurements and entanglements of city life. They constantly chant the Name of God and have great faith in saints and holy men.

Ramaiah Pillai was a Revenue Officer and a teacher. He was pious, virtuous and an ardent devotee of Lord Shiva. His wife Chinnammai, was also a noble woman endowed with wonderful qualities. On waking up every morning, both of them would bow down at the Lotus Feet of Mahadeva, also known as Nataraja in South India. They both would chant His Holy

Name with devotion and, as they did so, unbidden tears would trickle down their cheeks.

One day, a Sadhu knocked on the door of their house and said, "I am starving. Could you very kindly give me something to eat?"

The Sadhu's voice was sweet and on his face was a radiant smile. Chinnammai was profoundly moved by the appearance of the Sadhu. She said to herself, "I feel Lord Nataraj Himself has come in the form of this Sadhu to visit me."

She invited the holy man to sit down and served him with love and respect. "Please accept our offering," she said to him. "Today, we are most fortunate that, in your mercy, you have thought it fit to visit our humble abode." As she served him, tears flowed profusely from Chinnammai's eyes.

The Sadhu, seeing her devotion and deep love, accepted her offering (*biksha*) graciously. After having eaten, he blessed her, saying: "Mataji, I came to you as a stranger: you have showered on me love, respect and rich hospitality of the heart. In return, what can I offer you? I am but a mendicant, I have nothing to give you. But, I can give you this boon, that very soon, you will be blessed with a son like me."

The Sadhu blessed her and gave her Lord Shiva's *prasad* – sacred ash – before he left. As was their custom, Chinnammai smeared the holy ash on her forehead, and also ate a little of it.

The Sadhu's blessing came true – for she conceived soon thereafter. On October 5, 1823, a son was born to her; the child was named Rama Lingam.

When Rama Lingam was barely six years of age, tragedy struck the family. The father passed away suddenly, and the eldest son, Sabapati, took charge of the family.

As a child, Rama Lingam was a prodigy. He had an amazing memory. He was also loving and compassionate to all. He had deep love for God. He would often exclaim, "O Lord, You have given me this human birth. Bless me, that I may fulfill the purpose for which You have given it to me."

A vast majority of the people do not realise the value of the human birth. Alas, they fritter it away after useless things. They chase shadow-shapes which come and go. "Keep me away from the glitter and glamour of *Maya*," was this young child's constant prayer.

Child Rama Lingam would stay awake at night, shedding tears, communing with Lord Nataraj. Tears are a sign that our prayers arise from the depths of our hearts. Such prayers reach God straightaway. The prayers of many of us, arise from the superficies, the surface of our consciousness. They do not emerge from the depths of our hearts. Truly blessed is he who, while praying to God, sheds tears of love.

One special quality of child Rama Lingam was that he would talk very little. He never spoke in vain and his speech was always kind and sweet. If only we learnt this one lesson from his life – the lesson of speaking sparingly, sweetly, gently, kindly – our life too would be transformed. As it is, at the slightest pretext we get irritated, we lose our patience, we speak roughly with each other! Let us resolve to speak lovingly with one and all.

Sadhu Vaswani taught that the greatest *tapasya* is the *tapasya* of the tongue. It includes both taste and speech. For a little taste, we kill so many innocent creatures for food. The creatures, who are slaughtered everyday in our soulless cities, love life as much as we do. And we speak so many unnecessary words everyday – words of slander and cruel criticism.

It was Socrates, the great *yogi* of ancient Greece, who gave us three rules of speech. He would often say – "Before you want to say something, ask yourself three questions. If you get an answer in the affirmative to the three questions, you may speak. Otherwise, it is better that you hold your peace, and not utter a single word."

The first question, he said, is: before speaking, ask yourself: Is it *true*?

The second question is: Is it *necessary*? Is it going to be useful to anyone? If it is not necessary, then why utter it? Why waste energy unnecessarily?

The third question is: Is it *sweet*? Or will it hurt someone if, he hears it? If it is not sweet, it had better remain unuttered.

Is it true? Is it necessary and useful? Is it sweet? You will find that many of the words we utter are neither true, nor necessary, nor sweet.

We are told, that on an average, every person speaks about thirty thousand words, everyday. Out of those 30,000 words, how many will pass the triple test of Socrates? I am sure, very few. This realised Shri Rama Lingam, even when he was a child.

Rama Lingam grew to be a very intelligent boy. He had but to read something once, and it would be registered in his memory. His teachers loved him dearly. They would say to him, "Rama Lingam, your voice is so sweet. We love to hear you speak!" And Rama Lingam would say, "Sir, then join me in singing the *kirtan* of Nataraj. *Om Namo Shivaya! Bolo Om Namo Shivaya!*"

At the age of nine, he started composing poems in Tamil, in praise of the Lord. As Rama Lingam grew in years, he grew in love and devotion for the Lord. When he turned sixteen, he would frequently visit the Tiruvottyiyur Temple which had the idol of Thyagaraja. Rama Lingam established a loving relationship with God. He regarded God as His Father. He approached Him as a son would approach his father. This *bhava* is called *Pita-putra bhava*.

It is said, on one occasion, the Lord Himself took the form of a temple priest and came and fed Rama Lingam, who was starved and emaciated.

Rama Lingam did not wish to marry. But, much against his will, his elder brother forced him to do so. Even after his marriage, he lived a life of self-control and austerity. He had realised that the human birth was given us not for indulging in sense-pleasures, but for living a life of *sadhana*, self-discipline. Hence he made '*brahmacharya*' (celibacy) the rule of his life. Rama Lingam grew in spiritual awareness. Many people came to listen to his discourses.

One day, a rich disciple invited Rama Lingam to attend his daughter's wedding. Rama Lingam sent him a humorous reply in return. In the letter he wrote, "O, my heart, you have no shoes, nor a coat, nor beautiful clothes, nor any money, nor a pleasing personality. How then can you go to a rich man's wedding?"

Rama Lingam's thirst for a Vision of God grew, day by day. One day, while sitting in meditation, he had a vision in which he saw an ocean of Light, in which he took several dips. This, he named the Vast Grace-Light of the Divine, the Light of True Knowledge, which he called *Satya Jnana Jyoti*. He also heard a voice beckoning him, "You are My child. The thread of your life is in My Hands. Now go about and give the people the message of Love. Preach the gospel of Love and lead the people to the life that is noble and true and beautiful."

Rama Lingam followed the Call. He moved from village to village, from town to town, and gave the one message: Do not waste this precious human birth in eating, drinking, merry-making and sleeping. Life is meant for a higher purpose.

There was tremendous power in his words. People who heard him experienced a magical transformation in their hearts. He was able to instill the love of Truth in many hearts. He established a *Samarasa Veda Sanmarga Sanga* for the spread of spiritual knowledge. His life became a beacon light guiding many to the path of God-realisation.

One day, he called his devotees and said to them, "The time has now come when I will disappear. You will not be able to find me." And, so it happened. Rama Lingam Swami mysteriously disappeared. By this act of *siddhi*, he demonstrated to his followers the deathlessness of the *Atman*.

Till today, he remains alive in the hearts of his devotees. He would feed the poor and needy everyday, irrespective of caste, creed or colour. He also founded a school where the principles he preached were taught.

Rama Lingam Swami has passed away. But his teaching continues to live: "Stay away from lies and deception. Take truth to your hearts. Always remember that you have been given this body to realise God. Hence, stay away from sensual pleasures and instead embrace '*brahmacharya*' (celibacy). Control your senses. Speak less. Speak sweetly. Do not hurt anyone's feelings. Keep your mind one-pointed and focused. To achieve this, every day, meditate for a short while, because through meditation you can draw closer to God."

Rama Lingam Swami was a thinker, a writer, a gifted composer, and a healer in herbal medicines. His profound teachings are expressed in his six-volume work – *Thiru Arut Paa*.

These include:

1. Universal brotherhood
2. Equality of all souls
3. Self-discipline and control of the senses
4. Oneness of the Divine
5. *Ahimsa* – non-violence
6. Vegetarianism and
7. *Jeeva Karunya* – mercy to all creatures that breathe the breath of life.

Homage to Rama Lingam Swami! He taught us that the human birth has been given to us for a special purpose, and we will be able to fulfill this purpose by staying away from desires, by building our life in Truth, by staying away from violence, and by serving the sick, the poor, and animals and birds, thus making our lives worthwhile, beautiful and meaningful.

Sayings of Swami Rama Lingam

"Compassion is the key to the doors of Divine Grace."

* * * * *

"I am in this body. Henceforth, I would enter all the physical bodies."

* * * * *

"O Lord! Though hast given me the power to perform five-fold universal functions so that the multitudes of beings of the world shall get into the path of Light."

"My way is *Sanmarga* (the path of Truth, Right, Harmony and Purity) that abolishes death."

* * * * *

"I have received the Grace of the Lord who has brought me in this *yuga* or Age, so that I shall make all people of the world who are impure and dark within and even with a deceitful show of outward purity, get corrected or mended so as to join the way of *Sanmarga* and become happy by attaining life of the Heaven (i.e. a blissful life of deathless body) here itself."

* * * * *

"By the Grace of the Universal Lord of Truth-Knowledge even the shawl I wear will resurrect the dead into bodily life of flesh."

* * * * *

"I have got (the triple indestructible bodies of) *Suddha deha, Pranava deha* and *Jnana deha* in order to give myself freely in play everywhere(i.e. he wished to share his body's powers of transformation and deathlessness with others)."

Book by Swami Rama Lingam

- Six volumes of *"Arutpa"* (the poems of divine inspiration)

Some Books on Swami Rama Lingam

- *Life of Swami Ramalingam* – by T.V.G. Chetty
- *The Mother-Uno-Vallalar (Supramental Evolution Since 1874)* – by Sri T. R. Thulasiram
- *Vallalars' Vision of Nuclear Physics and the Nervous System* – Sri T. R. Thulasiram
- *Grace-Light: Universal Grace-Rule of Vallalar In His Radiant Deathless Body* – Sri T. R. Thulasiram

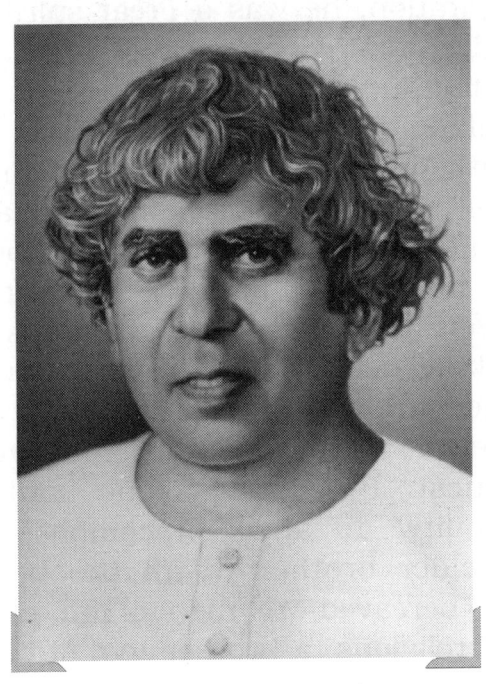

Sadhu Vaswani

Sadhu Vaswani was a modern day saint; he was a visionary idealist, a far-sighted educationist; he was a philosopher, a poet with heavenly inspiration; he was a great spiritual leader admired by men of light and leading in east and west; but all the adulation and fame he received sat lightly on him – for, he aspired to be a servant of the *sadhus*, *rishis* and saints of this ancient land; above all, he aspired to be a servant of suffering humanity. Thousands of seeking souls were drawn to him, eager to listen to every word he uttered, eager to obey his every request. But he was the soul of humility, an angel of compassion, an elder brother to all the bereft and bereaved, to men of all races and religions, a brother too, of birds and animals – a brother of all creation. He shared his all with all – the joy of his heart, the benedictions of his blessed life, the bliss of at-one-ment with God. For him, this was true *mukti*, true self-realisation – sharing with others the joy of the Eternal.

Sadhu Vaswani

*T*oday, 130 years after his birth, 57 years after he left Sind to live in India, Sindhis, Muslims and Hindus in Pakistan continue to revere Sadhu Vaswani, admire him and claim him as one of their own – as the greatest saint of 20th century Sind. Rarely has the world witnessed a brilliant intellect and a blazing spirit, manifested by as this saint from Sind.

How can I ever hope to describe my Gurudev to you in a manner befitting so great a saint as he?

Can a glow-worm describe the magic of the midnight moon? Can a candle set out in search of the bright noonday sun? Can a salt-doll fathom the depths of the ocean? Can a wayside flower speak of the beauty, the loveliness, the fragrance of the rose-gardens of Iran?

To be able to write of him I must have magic in my words and music in my heart – the music which makes life a hymn of dedication and love. And I must have within me a fire, a flame, burning ceaselessly, until it reduces all I have and all I am to naught!

I have neither the magic of words nor the music of the heart, and the spiritual flame has not yet been kindled within me. I but aspire to be an echo of the echo of his voice.

It rings in my ears like a temple bell. It whispers to me in the hours of silence. It speaks to me in my dreams. It wakes me up, gives me a shaking, until my whole frame begins to tremble like the wings of a frightened bird.

How long you will lie asleep, his voice doth ask, again and again. How long will you suffer in this world of vanity and vice? How long will you wander, chasing the shadow-shapes which come and go? How long will you, like children, fill your skirt with pebbles and pots with shells? Wake up! Wake up! And breaking the shackles of attachment to earthly life, move on to where your destiny calls you. The caravan is advancing. Listen to the camel-bells! What do they declare?

"O children of eternity!

You have rested long! 'Tis time to move on!"

An *Avatara* of Love Divine

"Children of Eternity!" The words are not idly spoken, they express the inner faith of his heart. Each one of us is a child of Eternity. Each one of us is a note in the Eternal song of the Lord. Alas! We identify ourselves with the frames of flesh and bone, with masks of matter and form, and we are carried away by every passing breeze of desire and fear, of anger and pride. Significant are the words of Sadhu Vaswani, "God is the Secret of man. Man never knows himself until he sees the God in himself. The deepest Self of man is God!"

And when we asked him, "If we be, indeed, of God, how is it we retain no recollection?" He answered, "The greased mirror cannot reflect aright. So the mind, clouded by desires and passions, obscures reflection of the great memory lying within the soul."

How may the mirror of the mind be cleansed of desires and appetites? Be drenched in love, is Sadhu Vaswani's answer. "Lose yourself in love," he says, "and you will find the One you seek!"

To be drenched in love, to lose oneself in love, is to walk, in Sadhu Vaswani's meaningful words, the "little way". And to walk the little way, is to become humble as dust, is to be emptied of the 'self' and all that the 'self' stands for – the clamour and confusion of our sordid, selfish, earthly existence.

If I were asked to express the secret of Sadhu Vaswani's life in a few words, I would sum it up in two words, humility and love. His humility defied description, and his boundless love moved out alike to the saint and the sinner, to the rich and the poor, to the great and the small, to men in power and to those whom the world tramples upon, everyday. Many of those who came in contact with him were wonder struck at his humility and love. One who met him for the first time, could not help but exclaim, "I have never received such love in all my life! Not even my parents, not even my children, have loved me as Sadhu Vaswani has done, during the few, brief minutes that I have spent in his soulful company!"

His humility was the humility of one who had reduced himself to naught. The deepest aspiration of his life was to become the 'lowest of the low'. Destiny dragged him, again and again, out of his solitude, to perform "great" things in life, but he always felt happy in doing little things. Great was his joy when he swept a room belonging to an "untouchable", and when he washed a beggar's body clean, clothing it in new garments. His face was lit up with joy as he sat at the grinding-stone making flour for feeding the poor. He felt inexpressibly happy when, out of his own hands, he fed the little birds that swarmed in hundreds, on the roof of his residence, at Karachi.

He Chose The 'Little Way'

Sadhu Vaswani rejoiced in the company of "little ones", the poor in Spirit. Not unoften he was asked by admiring friends to address big meetings and conferences. His invariable answer was, "Let the cobbler cobble his shoes!" In an answer to an invitation to take part in the "World Congress of Philosophers," he wrote: "I know nothing. A humbler task is the call to me of life."

To an age which worships at the altar of "greatness", Sadhu Vaswani, in his quiet way, showed what it was to be a "little one", to live a "hidden life in the Hidden God."

"What is your ambition?" he was asked by a press correspondent.

And Sadhu Vaswani answered, "I have no ambition. Every ambition is a chain which binds us to the earth. I but aspire to become a little one!"

The emphasis in his life was on being little. "In my hermit-heart," he said, "there sings, again and again, a little song: May I be as the little ones – the rose, the leaf, the lisping child!"

He taught by precept and example that greatness is a malady to be shunned. God asks not for great things, he said. Little things are precious to the Lord. In an age intoxicated with "ambition" and the mad rush for "bigness", Sadhu Vaswani's life rings with the message: "Sow little seeds of love and you will reap a rich destiny. Be a little one and through you He will reflect His Light – the Light of Eternity!"

Sufi Sind nourished him, nurtured him, and here in the land of his birth which he loved dearly, he evolved into the Angel of Love, the Messiah of Compassion, the Man of God, who is still venerated and revered in thousands of Sindhi homes all over the world.

The Master's Childhood

Even as a child, he was so different from other children. His face was beautiful to behold. And, again and again, his mother, who loved him dearly, would look long upon him and then, turning her eyes to the window, would gaze at the bright, blue sky, as if she saw visions. And as he grew in years, a far away look entered into his eyes. He became more and more aloof. He spent much of his time in solitude in an upper room which no one ever used.

Sometimes, as he sat to eat his meals and heard the cry of a passing beggar, he would take his food to share it with the hungry one. From the beginning, he was filled with the spirit of compassion which moved out to all who were suffering and in pain.

He did not play the games which the other children played. But he organised a little band of school children, who, each day, saved a little out of their pocket-money. The amount was then utilised in getting flour for making *chappaties* which he and his friends distributed among the crippled and the blind who sat on the wayside. And, as he saw their eyes sparkle with joy, he knew that loving service of the poor was, indeed, worship of God.

He was in the High School when a poor man came to him asking for a blanket. Before he could fetch his blanket, his teacher said to him, "Why give him the blanket? He will go and sell it. Give him instead a rupee coin and he will feel happy." Sadhu Vaswani, in a spirit of obedience, gave the poor man a rupee coin. The poor man went away happy, but Sadhu Vaswani said that he could not sleep the whole night, ashamed at not having given his blanket to a poor man in the cold of winter.

At night, he would sit on the house top and, for hours together, gaze in silent wonder, at the moon or the stars. On one such occasion, as he sat out in the moonlight, he saw, as in a "vision", a white figure with silvery hair and flowing beard. The figure called out to him and he answered the Call, and was lost in silence out of which he was awakened by his mother who carried him into the house. That was his first "vision", his first link with the unseen world and he was only eight years old. Ever since, he always felt that he was under the protection of an unseen force.

Pure Of Heart, Pure Of Spirit!

As a school-boy, he was brilliant at his studies and rarely missed the top rank. At the matriculation examination, he secured a scholarship which took him to college. His classmates in the college often wondered at the unsullied purity of his life and his utter guilelessness; they all loved and respected him, as one belonging to a world remote from their own.

One day, a few of his friends took him out for an evening walk. They were out for mischief. They took him to the house of a beautiful courtesan and, leaving the two together, disappeared for a while.

The courtesan gazed at him and her heart was inflamed, for he was truly handsome.

And she drew closer to him, the fragrance of her scented garments filled his nostrils. But he continued to sit still as a statue carved out of stone.

And she said to him in a bewitching voice, "Will you not step into my inner chamber?"

And he said, "Am I not already in the inner chamber?"

She did not understand the meaning of those words. Laying bare a part of her body, she said to him, "Look at me! Am I not truly beautiful?"

He looked not at her. But with eyes half-closed, he said to her, "Beloved sister! The beauty you behold in the mirror, again and again, will fade away sooner than you imagine, it is the beauty of flesh and skin. And flesh can draw only flesh to itself, and flesh becomes food for flesh and is consumed in the fire of passion. But there is another beauty which shall not fade! It is the beauty of the Unseen in you. Think of that beauty! Gaze upon it until your appetites are burnt and your body becomes a radiant temple of the Spirit."

The courtesan had never seen such a young man in all her life. She was speechless, lost in wonder.

Then, looking at her with his dawn eyes, he said, "Come, sister! Let us sing together the Holy Name of God!"

Amused, the courtesan joined in singing God's sacred Name. It was at that moment his friends entered the room, giggling, certain that they would behold their immaculate friend in the arms of the harlot. The joke was turned against them. And from that day, they knew Sadhu Vaswani was no ordinary person, that his life was incorruptible, stainless and pure as the flowing waters of the river Ganga, that he was of the race of those who visit the earth from time to time, but who do not belong to the earth. They belong to the Kingdom of Light, the Kingdom of the Spirit, the Kingdom that is higher than the stars and deeper than the seas.

A Brilliant Beginning

Sadhu Vaswani was born on November 25, 1879, in Hyderabad Sind, a land that has given birth to many *dervishes* (contemplatives) and *fakirs* (men of renunciation). He was a brilliant student, became an

"Ellis Scholar", and soon after doing his Masters, was appointed as Professor of History and English in the Vidyasagar College at Calcutta.

He was only thirty years of age when he went to Berlin as one of India's representatives to the *Welt Congress*, the World Congress of Religions. His speech there and his subsequent lectures in different parts of Europe aroused deep interest in Indian thought and religion and linked many with him in India's mission of help and healing.

His six months' stay in Europe, the reception he received there, the contacts he made with leaders of thought and culture in that great continent, enveloped him in a cloak of "greatness". So that when he returned to India, he said, he thought he was accorded more fame and adulation than he felt, he deserved. Whenever there was a big public function or meeting, he was asked to preside over it. He was not out for honours. "Honours and fame", he said to himself, "are chains, they fatten the ego." And the "ego" is the deadliest enemy of the pilgrim on the Path. Sadhu Vaswani promised himself not to preside over any meeting for a period of one year, by which time, he felt, the impression created by his European tour would be forgotten.

As he returned from Europe, he had with himself a heap of papers and journals in which his lectures had been reported and his articles published. One evening, as he paced to and fro on the deck of the steamer bringing him to India, a feeling came upon him that this, too, was vanity. The joy that a person got when he found his name in print could not be the true joy he was in search of. It was the joy of the ego-self that revels in pride and publicity. This joy must be crushed. And without a moment's hesitation, he went to his cabin and, taking out all the papers and journals, surrendered them to the waves of the sea.

Sadhu Vaswani did not keep a diary which would give us his life story, from where we could know more about his life.

He became Principal of more than one college. There was a brilliant career open to him, but he was still young, barely forty, when his mother died. He had given a pledge to his mother that he would not renounce the world and become a *fakir*, so long as she was alive. Now when his mother died, he felt that his bonds were broken. He was free as the breeze which bloweth where it listeth. The very first thing that he did, after his mother's funeral, was to send in his resignation. His friends urged him not to be in a hurry to give up his job.

"Why do you give up your lucrative job?" they said to him. "You are still young, you have a bright future before you, you can make money, heaps of money."

"Life is not given to make money," he replied.

"What then is the purpose of life?" they asked him.

And he answered, "To dedicate it to Love Divine, to serve and be poured out as a sacrifice."

His Role In The Freedom Struggle

Sadhu Vaswani's contribution to the freedom struggle, was, indeed significant. As far as Sind was concerned, he was the foremost interpreter, and in India, one of the earliest advocates of Mahatma Gandhi's Non-Cooperation Movement. In that early period, Sadhu Vaswani took on the task of promoting the new movement. At the Sind Political Conference of the Indian National Congress, he was the one to move the resolution on the policy and programme of Non-cooperation. In fact, it was thanks to his stature and influence that the resolution was carried and passed, in the teeth of united opposition from veteran Sindhi leaders! Thanks to Sadhu Vaswani, Sind was pledged to Mahatma Gandhi's Movement.

Sadhu Vaswani genuinely believed that the *Satyagraha* movement would spiritualise the life of India's people. This belief, this aspiration, is reflected in the many books he wrote at that time, including *India Arisen, Awake, Young India!, India's Adventure, India in Chains, The Secret of Asia, My Motherland, Builders of Tomorrow* and *Appostles of Freedom*. These inspiring books exhorted Indians, especially the youth, to dedicate their lives to the service of the Motherland.

Alas! Mass movements often tend to lose touch with the mind and the spirit; and their integrity is often compromised by utilitarianism. It made Sadhu Vaswani grieve, to see some of the patriots of the freedom-movement, scramble for power and position. He himself idealised Kagawa and Sonotoku, who flatly refused to accept salaries, when they were offered senior government positions. He would often quote their powerful and unanswerable question: "Why should men who want to help their country receive a salary for doing so?" He believed, with them, that leaders should, first and foremost, be *servants* of the people, and live as the poorest among the poor, giving all their time and energy to serving the country.

He worked for Swaraj; he sang of India's freedom – and he was saddened to see one bureaucracy replaced by another. He wanted above all, that in our struggle for freedom, we must be true to the spirit of humanity.

"What is your politics?" he was asked. He replied, "My politics, you ask? *Service of the poor*, is my answer, in brief. The divine urge of freedom cannot be killed. It must grow from more to more. A state is not free until the poor have come into their own. How may we build such a state? The problem is beyond politics."

For years together, he kept on sounding a note of warning – that if, in our enthusiasm for political freedom, we neglect *other aspects* of freedom – social, cultural and spiritual – politics will fail in its purpose, and the nation will only wander from darkness to darkness. Alas, this became painfully true in the years following our independence.

This is why he turned to work for Youth Movements. His aim was to train youth, to harness their *shakti* for the service of India. He believed in the youth, as the destined leaders of the nation, and wanted them to be trained and disciplined, in order to fulfil their role in the great task that awaited them. To his last, he believed that the true work of Freedom, was, as yet, incomplete in India.

The Many Facets Of The Master

Sadhu Vaswani also gave his attention to education and other spheres, emphasising that character-building is nation-building. He started 'Youth Centres' in different places. He opened the "Shakti Ashram" at Rajpur, inspired by faith in the youths of India. He founded the Mira Movement in Education which today has its headquarters at Pune. This Movement aims at unfolding a new renaissance of culture. And so students in St. Mira's Educational Institutions are given a triple training of the head, the hand and the heart. Education is regarded as essentially a thing of the Spirit. And the truth is emphasised that the end of all knowledge is service – service of the poor and lowly, the sick and the afflicted ones.

Sadhu Vaswani's life has been one of unceasing service and sacrifice. He worked day after day, wanting nothing for himself, seeking only opportunities to serve the poor, the lowly and the lost. At the advanced age of seventy-nine, his body became weak, but he felt that he had the "strength of ten" because in his heart was love and every fibre of his being thrilled with faith in man and God.

Sadhu Vaswani's teaching, in brief, was that in the love of God and the service of His suffering children (birds and animals too, are His children), was the secret of true life. He believed in the unity of races and religions, in the One Spirit. His heart rose in reverence to all saints and prophets of East and West. "My religious philosophy," he said, "is theomonistic. My reverence for Krishna and the Buddha and Christ and Nanak is too deep for words. And I have learnt, not without some study and meditation, to salute Muhammad among the Prophets of God."

And again, "There are so many who can believe only one thing at a time. I am so made as to rejoice in the many and behold the beauty of the One in the many. Hence my natural affinity to many religions. In them all I see revelations of the One Spirit. And deep in my heart is the conviction that I am a servant of all Prophets."

His life was radiant with the great truth of fellowship with all creation. "The creation of God," he said, "is bound by golden chains to the feet of the One God, the One Divine Father of us all."

At His Lotus Feet we all are one, men of different religions and no religion. No one is an alien in the Kingdom of God. And Sadhu Vaswani's earnest advice to all seekers on the Path is to limit themselves to no one scripture but to regard all scriptures as receptacles of spiritual wisdom. For all do flow from the one Fount of Inspiration. To Sadhu Vaswani, therefore, all sectarian strifes and quarrels in the name of religion were born of ignorance, illusion, *maya*.

In Sadhu Vaswani's life, as in his teaching, the emphasis is on detachment. "Conquer *trishna*, desire!" is the note he has sounded again and again. And in his daily life, detachment was blended with love and compassion for all – for sinners and criminals, for the "fallen" and forsaken ones, and birds and animals. He could never bear the sight of suffering and pain, it spurred him to action and would not let him rest, until he had done something to alleviate the agony of his fellow-beings.

The Messiah Of Compassion

The essential quality of his life, as it has seemed to me, through the many years that it had been my undeserved privilege to be near him, was his divine compassion and tenderness for all those whom the cruel world tramples upon day after day. I was with him during the few days that he was sent to the Karachi Jail for having launched a *Satyagraha* campaign for a socio-religious cause. I saw with what tenderness he met thieves and murderers, sinners and "criminals". On learning that a "man of God" was their fellow-guest, they came to him, they beheld in his eyes the light of a brother, and they opened out their hearts to him, making a clear confession of the crimes they had committed. And often their eyes and the eyes of Sadhu Vaswani glistened with unbidden tears. "They are my friends and brothers," Sadhu Vaswani said to me. "And to them I fain would reveal the boundless love and mercy of God."

Deep in his heart, there was the conviction that there is neither sin nor sinner. There is only God and His manifestations, His children, standing at different stages of evolution, all struggling to reach the Goal. "There is, a treasure God giveth in darkness, and sinners are nearer to the Kingdom of Love than the self-righteous." His Daily Prayer was radiant with the following moving words:

"O Lord! Have mercy on them whom men have made criminals by denying them work and bread and then, in their hunger and humiliation, have chained them in jails!"

"O Lord! Dry the tears of them whom humanity hath not heeded and hath made harlots, too weak to resist the tempter and the tyrant!"

His compassion was not restricted to human beings. It extended to all creatures, even to trees and flowers. He would not pluck flowers, for flowers, as he said, had their families, and they must not be separated from each other. So he did not accept flower-garlands. The quality of his soul was clearly revealed, also, in his treatment of animals. He could not resign himself to the sufferings of animals at the cruel hands of the butcher. "For me not to love bird and animal would be not to love the Lord," he said. "For His children are birds and animals, no less than human beings."

In the compound of St. Mira's High School was a shed; it was the dwelling place of a few lambs and goats, a cow and cocks rescued by Sadhu Vaswani from the jaws of death as they were being driven to the slaughter house. "No price is too great to save a single life!" he said to me once. It is on such occasions that his large crystal eyes sparkled with a light which is not seen on land or sea. And, as I looked into the depths of that wondrous light, I had involuntarily exclaimed, "Are you Sadhu Vaswani or are you God?"

The Power Of His Words

Sadhu Vaswani was a born orator. He made his first public speech when he was only fifteen years old. He delivered thousands of lectures. It was as a schoolboy that he knew that God had endowed him with the gift of speech. He was walking along the bank of the river Phuleli in Hyderabad Sind, when he suddenly felt like speaking. He "lisped in numbers and the numbers came." He recollected the first words of his speech made on the river bank with no one to listen to him but the flowing waters and the solitary trees: "I come to you with faith and love in my heart."

Sadhu Vaswani spoke but little. On every Sunday evening, he addressed a large meeting of men and women who gathered together at the St. Mira's Hall, in a beautiful spirit of faith and devotion. They heard him and marvelled at his words. He awakened new aspirations in the hearts of many who listened to him. When he spoke, he filled the hall with the rich music of his words and the richer music of his heart.

He was a prolific writer, in English and in the sweet lyrical Sindhi language. In his writings an unknown world unfolds itself before us, new dimensions fill us with unbounded wonder, profound and startling truths are revealed to us with a simplicity and beauty that is unrivalled. Many have spoken to me, of the deep, penetrative quality of his words. Many have written to me, from different parts of the world, of the depth and height and vastness his writings have added to their consciousness.

Without the least exaggeration, I may say that his words, both spoken and written, have again and again transported me to a new world of truth and beauty and radiance. I know that my life, and my death, would be richer, nobler, and more serene than they would have otherwise been. His contribution to the world of letters and culture is great, his writings have a stamp of immortality upon them, and will, I have no doubt, continue to be a rich source of comfort and spiritual consolation to generations unborn. "Which is Sadhu Vaswani's best book?" was the question put to me by a retired Principal, the other day. I smiled as I answered, "Sadhu Vaswani's best book is an unwritten book." For his greatest masterpiece was not written with pen on parchment, but with his life on the tablets of our hearts.

Great as were his mental powers, rich his knowledge, wisdom and intuition concerning different spheres of life, his true sphere was that of the Spirit. Living in the midst of humanity, he lived as one apart, for he lived in the world of the Spirit. And something, a spiritual influence, streamed out of him in a perennial flow. It is that which cast a spell upon all who drew near him. When he entered a room, all hearts were hushed. When he opened his mouth, men and women hung on to his words. And no wonder! For his words were not the words of an ordinary human being. They were the words of one who had been charged to deliver the message of the Lord of Life, Light, and Love in this world of darkness and tears.

Thinking of him and the stainless purity of his life, of his humility and love, of his spirit of detachment blended with compassion, of the flame of divine life that burned ceaselessly within him, of the smile that oft played upon his lips and the sadness that lay in the depths of his eyes, the sadness of all the world, I had whispered to myself, again and again:

In all the world
There is scarce another
Like unto Thee!
Thou art the mountain-peak:
I am a frail climber!
Thou art the ever-loving mother:
I am a child lost
In the fair of this world!
And yet this have I learnt of Thee,
That I am Thy yesterday,
Thou art my tomorrow.
I am a tiny stream:
Thou art the rushing torrent.
And if only I flow into Thee,
Together we shall move on
And become one in Him
Who is the End
And fulfillment of life!

Sadhu Vaswani And Sind

From 1929, he came to live in Hyderabad Sind, his birthplace. It was here that his richest spiritual contributions to Sind unfolded. He took upon himself the task of spreading the word of God, and the message of India's ancient Hindu scriptures. The Brahmo Mandir, the Guru Sangat, the Bawa Ishwardas Temple and the Theosophical Society Hall, reverberated to the inspiring and uplifting power of his illumined discourses.

Nor were his efforts confined to addressing the intellectual elite of Sind. He started Gita classes and Sunday classes where men and women from all walks of life could come and participate in reading, reciting and listening to the holy scriptures. He began Blue Bird Classes, where women could learn the English language and also get to hear about the lives of great women.

Here too, in Sind, he contributed to the revival of the Vedic religion, moving away from rite-and-ritual bound customs, dominated by priests. In the narrow lanes of Hirabad, he single-handedly revived the New Bhakti Movement, with *naam sankirtan* resounding in the streets, and *prabhat pheri* in the sacred hours of the dawn.

To the mystic, majestic Sindhi language and its magnificient literature, Sadhu Vaswani's contribution has truly been invaluable. Poet, prophet, philosopher, inspired writer and gifted orator, every word that he uttered and every sentence that he wrote are worthy enough to be inscribed in indelible letters of immortality.

Perhaps no other writer, no other spiritual leader has written so extensively on the great Ones of East and West. He studied their lives, imbibed the best of their teachings and shared the essence of their wisdom with one and all, through his inspired discourses and brilliantlly written works. He wrote with equal fervour of Jesus Christ and Prophet Muhammad; of Gautama Buddha and Mahavira; of Kabir and Chaitanya; of Rabia and Mira; of Guru Nanak and Sri Ramakrishna; of Adi Shankara and St. Francis; of Tukaram and St. Augustine – of scores of saints and sages, belonging to all countries, races and religions.

His *Nuri Granth* is outstanding work judged by any literary standard. It is a collection of over 4000 songs and 2000 *slokas* – perhaps the longest and greatest work of a single poet-saint in any language in the world. Its poetic merit is of a high order; its lyricism is exquisite; its emotional appeal is profound; its spiritual intensity is powerful. But as a divinely inspired work of devotion, it is unsurpassed. Truly, it is a work reserved for immortality.

Feminism, women's liberation and the empowerment of women have become empty, clichéd expressions now. In the days before the word feminism was even coined, Sadhu Vaswani offered the *purdah*-clad, kitchen-bound women of Sindh, *spiritual liberation* in the true sense of the term. His *Sakhi Satsang* enabled many women to become decision-makers for the first time in their personal lives – by the very act of voluntarily joining his *satsang*. It would be no exaggeration to say that he inducted Sindhi women into what had until then been the domain of men – the *practise* of religion in the true sense.

He did everything he could to break the shackles of superstition and hidebound 'customs' that had kept

Sindhi women restricted and confined for centuries. He spoke out against the *purdah* as also against the deadly custom of *deti-leti* (dowry). At the same time, he was also aware of the dangers of excessive 'modernism', warning women against aping western fashions blindly. He encouraged them to cultivate the virtue of simplicity in their dress and in their daily life.

The *Sakhi Satsang* was quite revolutionary in its spiritual, social, cultural and economic impact on Sindhi women, if one were to consider the movement in all its aspects. For the first time, women learnt about economic independence, accountability and trust, when they were given the management of *Sakhi Stores*. They took their first steps on the path of self-reliance, outside the secure confines of their own homes.

At the *Sakhi* Conference organised by him for their benefit, they had the chance to make themselves heard on matters concerning themselves; on social evils like dowry, child marriage and exploitation. Sadhu Vaswani's *Seva Ashram* opened a new world to women who wished to tread the spiritual path. Above all, he emphasised the spiritual *shakti* of women, exclaiming aloud to the male-dominated society, "The woman-soul shall lead us, upward, on!"

Sadhu Vaswani's contribution to Education was equally significant. The MIRA movement in education, which he founded in Hyderabad Sind, set new standards for value-based education which emphasised character development and cultivation of the soul. His ideal of the triple training of the head, the hand

and the heart added a new dimension to the education of girls. His innovative practices did not end there. For the first time in modern Sind, he offered hostel facility to girls who could not have access to good education in the vicinity of their homes. When he founded Mira College in Sind, he had it affiliated to the Banaras Hindu University, arranging to escort the girl students with appropriate chaperonage and security to Benaras, for their University exams.

Believing as he did that "service of the poor was worship of God", Sadhu Vaswani exhorted his ever-growing band of volunteers and devotees to concentrate their efforts towards improving the lot of the needy and underprivileged. He started a *Modikhana* after the manner of Guru Nanak, to provide basic necessities to the poor. Making a humble start to his Medical Welfare service programme by visiting poor patients in hospitals to distribute food and fruits to them, he actually succeeded, even in those early days, in setting up a dispensary at the *Sakhi Satsang* premises, which gave free treatment to poor patients.

Today, The Sadhu Vaswani Mission's Medical Complex in Pune has no less than four fully equipped state-of-the-art hospitals. The day is not far off, when a MIRA University will take shape. Sadhu Vaswani Centres all over the world are humbly and earnestly carrying on the noble task of translating their Master's ideals into reality. But nothing can equal the pioneering spirit and the devotional zeal with which Sadhu Vaswani began his life's work of service to society and humanity in those early days, in the land so dearly beloved to him!

The light that dawned in Hyderabad-Sind now shines bright all over the sub-continent, and indeed in the four corners of the world. The Sadhu Vaswani Mission, named after the Saint of Sind, still adds glory and luster to the land of Sufis and Saints that he called his own Sun-lit Sind:

> This day I think, again, of thee, of thee –
> Beloved of this broken, lonely heart!
> My Native Land of mystic Song and art!
> Thou soil of lyric stars and Singers Three!
> My Sufi Sind!
> My Sun-Lit Sind!
> This day I think of brothers mine: they weep:
> Of sisters mine: they cry for bread and home:
> I think of all who homeless still do roam
> And when the night doth come, on the road side sleep!
> My Sufi Sind!
> My Sun-Lit Sind!
> Thy children there: O who will give them hope
> And food and shelter, help, and health to bear
> Their lot in loneliness – to bear and dare
> To build again, e'en tho' in darkness they grope!
> My Sufi Sind!
> My Sun-Lit Sind!
> I see around me darkness, suffering, woe:
> The light of hope has died in many hearts;
> I see, alas! That faith in God departs:
> And hungry children cry where'er I go!
> My Sufi Sind!
> My Sun-Lit Sind!

Sayings of Sadhu Vaswani

"Love, love, love even thine enemy; and though he hate thee as a thorn, thou wilt blossom as a rose."

* * * * *

"O Lord of Life and Light! Bless me by breaking me! And break me to make me new! Make me a child of Love!"

* * * * *

"Purity is the best pilgrimage; and the best prayer is the healing of a broken heart."

* * * * *

"The world is on flames: and what power can quench them if not the power of love?"

* * * * *

"All world-religions are mirrors of the One Face. In them all, shines the One Light."

* * * * *

"For me not to love bird and animal would be not to love the Lord. For, His children are birds and animals, no less than human beings."

* * * * *

"The finest flower of civilisation is freedom: this grows on the soil of reverence for life."

* * * * *

"Life's richest treasure is the loving heart that is at peace with all."

* * * * *

"One Light in all Religions!
One Inspiration in all Scriptures!
One Wisdom in all Sages!"

* * * * *

"Not in the clamour of crowds and strife for the things which are passing, but in being *still*, is the pure joy of life."

Some Books by Sadhu Vaswani

- Nuri Granth (In Sindhi, Devnagari Script and English Translation)
- The Bhagavad Gita: The Song of Life (with Sanskrit Slokas)
- The Bhagavad Gita: The Song of the Supreme
- The Heart of the Gita
- Discover Yourself!
- Pilgrimage to God
- Lights From Many Lanterns
- Sufi Saints of East & West
- Thus Have I Learnt
- Breakfast With God
- The Life Beautiful
- Heart Beats
- Kindle the Light
- Heroes of History
- The Voice of the Voiceless
- Guru Nanak: Prophet of Peace
- Masters and Mystics
- The Call of New Education
- All Life is Sacred
- Sind and the Sindhis
- Golden Gleamings
- Call of Mira Education
- The Voice of Vaswani

Some Books on Sadhu Vaswani

- Sadhu Vaswani: His Life and Teachings – by J. P. Vaswani
- A Day With Sadhu Vaswani – by J. P. Vaswani
- A Saint of Modern India – by Hari P. Vaswani

Gurudev Ranade

Gurudev Ranade was a rare soul – an eminent scholar, a brilliant academic, who turned to the life spiritual and attained illumination through divine grace. A professor who became a prophet, Gurudev Ranade rose above book learning to reach salvation through single-minded pursuit of the truth. His distinguished position as a Vice Chancellor and an eminent Professor of Philosophy, did not distract him from his spiritual aspirations. With the simple *sadhana* of meditation, the practise of daily silence and repetition of the Name Divine, he attained great spiritual heights, and showed the way to thousands of his followers.

Gurudev Ranade

Gurudev Ranade was a great scholar, a gifted author, a highly learned man. In the history of humanity, there have been very few academics, who have attained spiritual illumination. Gurudev Ranade was one of them. He was a man of books who attained divine bliss through spiritual wisdom. He was a scholar, who became a saint. He was a professor, who became a prophet.

As a rule, scholars and learned men do not long for God-realisation. Their vast knowledge confines them to books and research. But Gurudev Ranade was different from other academics. In fact, he did write many books. But his ultimate attainment was far above mere book-learning.

He was born on July 3, 1886, at Jamkhandi, in Bijapur District. His mother brought him up in a holy atmosphere. He was a very humble student; he had great reverence for his teachers, as well as for his fellow-students.

He worked very hard, studying late into the nights. But he felt disheartened because, try as he might, he could never secure the highest marks in his class. "I work so hard on all my subjects," he thought to himself, "why is it that I do not top my class? Let me find out from the student who comes first every time, what he does that is different, which enables him to top the class, whereas I cannot."

One day, he decided to follow the boy who always topped the class. He saw that before this boy went to school, he visited a temple and bowed down before the *moorti*, offered prayers and after seeking blessings proceeded to school. From that day onwards, Gurudev Ranade, whose name was Ram Chander, also started the same practice.

Soon thereafter, Ram Chander realised his ambition – he stood first in his class... As it is, he was well-mannered and his behaviour towards his fellow-students was friendly and polite. He was always ready to help people. Hence, most of the students liked him a lot and held him in high regard. Now, as a topper, his teachers appreciated him even more. There were a few students in the school who did not like the special treatment given to him and were jealous of him.

There was a student who was given to the habit of smoking. One day, he collected all the butt ends of the cigarettes he had smoked, and slyly placed them in Ram Chander's pocket! Ram Chander was not aware of what had happened.

The student then suggested to the teacher: "Sir, kindly check the pockets of all students; by doing so you will know the true character of the students. You will also come to know what is going on these days in the school. After all, appearances can be deceptive. We all look so good and kind and well-mannered, but you will only get to know the truth when you check each one of us out."

The students agreed to this and let the teacher search each and everyone. It was Ram Chander's turn and, sure enough, his pockets were found to be full of cigarette butts. The teacher was shocked. He said, "You are too young for all this. I am truly disappointed with you! I always took you to be an ideal student who lived a regulated life. Truly, I held you in high regard and loved you more than my own son. What is this that you have been doing? Smoking cigarettes? I cannot believe my eyes!" The teacher was very upset and angry and punished Ram Chander severely.

On that day, Ram Chander said to himself, "I must learn from this experience; I will not ever blame anyone until I am convinced of the truth beyond all doubt."

The teacher thought that Ram Chander was caught red-handed. But the truth was known only to Ram Chander and the student who played the trick. Ram Chander said to his teacher, "Sir, it is only God, I and the one who has played this trick who know the truth. I can only swear that I have never smoked a cigarette."

When Ram Chander was preparing for his school finals, he came in contact with a holy man, named Bhau Saabh Maharaj. When Ram Chander met this saint, he felt that he should take a *mantra*, and be initiated by him. He therefore requested the holy man to grant him the *Naam mantra*. Before doing so, he begged the saint, "Swamiji, pray tell me, by taking this *Naam mantra*, will I be able to attain higher knowledge? Will it help me to make progress on the spiritual path? I am in search of salvation."

Bhau Saabh Maharaj, himself was not a learned man. He said to the boy, "You must practise silence every day. Therefore, you must choose a silence corner and, without fail, sit there every day, preferably at the same time, and chant the sacred *mantra* with deep love and longing, and you will attain the knowledge you are seeking."

Gurudev Ranade said later, "This is how I entered on the path. Every day, without fail, I practised silence and tried to enter within." Before the saint gave the *Naam mantra* to Ram Chander, he made him take three vows. Firstly, he made him promise that he would observe and practise the repetition of the *mantra*, everyday. Secondly, that he would never desire any other person's wealth. And thirdly, that he would consider another man's wife as his mother.

Ram Chander came from a small village. In spite of this, at the matriculation examination – which was a University examination – he stood first in Sanskrit language. He was awarded a scholarship which enabled him to get admission to the Deccan College in Pune.

The village boy had to move to the city. His mother who loved him more than words may tell, had tears in her eyes when he took leave of her. His mother was a pious lady. We are told that when he was in the mother's womb, every day she would find time to sit in a silence corner and do *Naam jap* and invoke benedictions on the child to be born. Little wonder, she was blessed with a son who guided many a pilgrim on the pathway to God.

In 1914, Ram Chander passed the M.A. examination with full honours. He was appointed as a Professor in the Fergusson College. He wrote books on pathways to God which continue to help seekers whose hearts aspire to the True, the Good, the Beautiful.

Gurudev Ranade delivered lectures on Upanishadic philosophy, on the *Bhagavad Gita*, on the Vedanta. His first monumental work was *The Constructive Survey of Upanishadic Philosophy*, published in 1926. It brought him fame and he was invited to join the Allahabad University as a Professor. He rose to become the head of the Philosophy Department, and attained to the eminent position of a Vice-chancellor. He never felt proud of his attainments but continued to be as humble as ever. He attended to his academic duties faithfully, but never lagged behind in pursuing his spiritual practices.

After his retirement, he lived in an *ashram* he had built at Nimbal, a small village, near Solapur. Many seekers became his devout disciples, and attended his *satsangs* at Nimbal.

In 1909, Gurudev Ranade fell ill with tuberculosis which, in those days was considered an incurable disease. He was bedridden for many days and suffered physical pain: but on his lips there was always a soft smile and in his heart a prayer of thanksgiving. He continued to recite from the *Bhagavad Gita* every day. "The Gita is my daily medicine," he would say.

A day came when, after his morning meditation was over, he called his devotees and asked them to perform *aarati*. In the *aarati* they burnt camphor as they chanted *Vithal Vithal*. When the camphor flame was extinguished, some of the disciples saw the soul departing from the body of their beloved Gurudev Ranade.

Gurudev Ranade had written a letter to one of his friends a few days earlier. In the course of the letter he wrote, "Our only pursuit should be to follow the Will of God, and meditate on Him. If we do this, He will come to our aid in all circumstances."

Gurudev Ranade laid emphasis on two things. The first is, at every step, in every round of life, we must learn to accept the Will of God. Let this be the *mantra* of our life: "Not my will but Thy Will be done, O Lord!" The second is, each day, we must meditate on God. This will draw us closer to the Lotus Feet of God where alone is true love and joy and peace.

Acceptance of the Will of God and meditation on His Form and Name: those two things made Gurudev Ranade the great soul that he was. By performing simple *sadhanas*, he rose to great spiritual heights. However, he was constant in his practice; he fulfilled the vow that he had made to his Guru, years ago.

May Gurudev Ranade's life and teaching be a perennial source of inspiration to us all!

Sayings of Gurudev Ranade

"It would not be possible for any one to meet God until one's egoism is at an end."

* * * * *

"There is only one favour that we should ask of God: that we should always think of Him in our heart; that we should always utter His Name by our mouth; that we should always see Him with our eyes; that our hands should worship only Him; that our head be placed always at His feet; that our ears should only hear of God's exploits; that He should show Himself always to our right and to our left, before and after, and at the end of our life. We should ask God for no other favour except this."

* * * * *

"As trees do not know honour and dishonour, as they are equal to those who worship them and those who cut them, similarly, the saints in their supreme courage look upon honour and dishonour alike."

* * * * *

"Him alone we may call a saint," says Namadeva, "who sees God in all beings; who looks upon gold as a clod of earth; who looks upon a jewel as a mere stone; who has driven out of his heart anger and passion; who harbours peace and forgiveness in his mind; whose speech is given merely to the utterance of God's Name."

* * * * *

"There is neither time nor season for the meditation of God. There is neither a high caste nor low in His meditation. He who is the Ocean of love and pity shall come to the succour of all."

* * * * *

"Mountains of sin shall perish in an instant at the utterance of the Name of God."

Some Books by Gurudev Ranade

- Constructive Survey Of Upanishadic Philosophy
- Mysticism In Maharashtra
- Pathway to God In Hindi Literature
- Parmarth Sopan
- The Conception Of Spiritual Life In Mahatma Gandhi and Hindi Saints
- The Bhagvatgita As A Philosophy Of God Realisation
- Pathway To God In Kannada Literature
- Paramartha Mandira
- Essays And Reflections
- The Vedanta As A Culmination Of Indian Philosophical Thought

Some Books on Gurudev Ranade

- *Religion and the changing world: The predicament of man* (Gurudev Ranade memorial lectures) – by P. Nagaraja Rao
- *Autobiography of Gurudev R.D. Ranade: A discovery* – by Vinayak Chintaman Kelkar
- *The role of Sri Krishna in the Mahabharata* (Gurudev Ranade memorial lectures) – by Ke. Es. Narayanacharya

Jose Rizal

Jose Rizal was an extraordinary young man – a fiery revolutionary and a devout Christian, he made it his life's mission to free his motherland Philippines, from the bonds of slavery and colonial repression. A qualified doctor, an eye specialist, Rizal was deeply interested in philosophy and theology, and made up his mind, even as a young man, that he would lay his life down for the sake of his beloved country. An inspired poet, his words were the trumpet call that awakened thousands of his countrymen to fight for their independence. Rizal became a martyr for the cause – but his untimely death was not in vain, for his dream became a reality, and he himself became an icon of patriotism and nationalism to his people.

Jose Rizal

"Pretty little lady, you dazzle me with your dance! I have never ever seen such dancing, before," said the Governor-General of the Philippine Islands to a little girl. "Allow me to give you a present. Tell me what shall it be?"

"Give me back my mother from prison," the girl replied instantly.

"Who is the girl's mother? Set her free, whoever she is," commanded the Governor-General.

And so the little girl's mother was released. She had been falsely accused and sent to prison because of the vengeance of a Spanish lieutenant, whom her husband had prevented from trampling on their fields. She had been falsely accused of conspiring to kill a Mrs. Rolando whom she would have never ever dreamt of hurting.

In fact, the little girl who danced her way into the governor's heart was a *little boy* of eleven – Jose Rizal—who had felt the sting of slavery, very early in life. That sting went deep into his heart.

Thousands of mothers and fathers like his own, and very many children were being treated cruelly, every day, by their colonisers. The Philippine Islands were, at that time, almost forgotten remnants of the Spanish empire. That empire, corrupt and decrepit, was governed from far-off Madrid, so that actually most of the power lay in the hands of the incorrigible local Catholic Church and a few Spanish landowners who misused it thoroughly. A word from them would send hundreds into prison or exile.

As Rizal thought of the pitiable condition of his country, the picture that came before him was the picture of his people being insulted and despised, of children being rendered homeless and friendless. It was a picture of desolation and despair! The picture penetrated into the depths of his soul. He felt that a call had come to him – clear and straight – a call from his Motherland. And in answer to the call, he resolved to lay down his life for the cause of his country's independence.

As he was very young, he felt that he had to wait and prepare for his great task, and not act in a hurry. He would learn all there was to be learnt and more. And when he grew up, he would plan his strategy and set out to fulfill the dream of his life.

He subjected himself to a hard, rigorous life, disciplining the body and the mind, by following a strict daily regimen. He did not smoke, did not drink wine and avoided keeping awake late at night. He wasted no time in being idle, and saved his energy to prepare himself for the tremendous task he had assigned to himself.

When he was just eighteen years of age, one of his poems, "To the Philippine Youth", won the first prize in the Manila Lyceum of Arts and Literature.

Spanish officials were shocked and questioned: who was the insolent young man, who had the impudence to dream of any motherland other than Spain?

Then the students of the Ateneo de Manila enacted a play called, "Beside the Pasig". In the play, the devil was made to impeach Spain for her cruelty. Was Spain so rotten that even the devil denounced her? Who had the courage to write such a play? Who was this traitor? Again, it was Jose Rizal!

Men had been sent to the gallows for very minor "crimes". But what of this? The Philippines was no longer safe for him. Money was collected and a passport was obtained under a false name for him. And so one midnight, Jose slipped out in a boat which was bound for Spain. There he would be safe, for Spain was a hundred times freer than its colonies.

At Madrid, he studied Medicine and specialised in the treatment of the diseases of the eye. He utilised his leisure hours in studying literature, philosophy, French, German and English.

On completion of his course in Medicine, he went to Paris where he practised with a famous eye specialist.

He devoted himself to his profession during the day and parts of his nights to writing his first book, *Noli Me Tangeri*, which in Latin means, "Touch Me Not". After two years the book was ready. It was the story of Ibarra, a desperate revolutionary, who was immediately recognised as Rizal himself by those who knew him. Ibarra's father drew a parallel to Rizal's imprisoned mother. Every character in the book was easily recognised by the people of Calamba, his hometown. The book received a tremendous response. William Dean Howells, the famous American writer and critic, appraised it as the best book that had been written in any language for fifty years.

For the first time, the Spanish friars saw themselves being looked upon with contempt. For the first time, people had dared to stand up and be defiant towards them. The book was proscribed. A decree was issued restraining Filipinos from handling the book; offenders were threatened with exile and confiscation of land and property, while rewards were announced for the people who reported such offenders.

The decree produced the contrary effect. It did not prevent the people from reading the book. It aroused their curiosity and urged them to discover for themselves the contents of the book which had shaken in such a large measure, the confidence of their rulers. The books were smuggled into Manila; people read the book by lamplight in hiding and, after reading, passed it on to others. A ripple was created all through

Philippine Islands and for the first time, something like a mass awakening took hold of the Filipinos. Jose Rizal became the most famous man in the Philippines.

After some time he dared to come to his hometown, Calamba, for the sake of his mother who was going blind. For the first time in Philippine history, he successfully performed a very delicate operation on her. He came to be known as a miracle-man. Patients came to him from the very remote corners of the Island and even from China and Japan. His stay in Calamba was short, because after six months, he was advised by the Governor-General to leave the Islands, as there were rumours that attempts would be made to kill him. The advice was actually more a threat and an order; so Rizal departed.

He went to America, but in his absence, his family was brutally treated. He returned to Madrid. But there was little he could do. The authorities would not listen to him. Full of bitterness, he wrote a book called, *El Filibusterismo*.

He was imprisoned and sent to Mindanao. For four years he was there; he converted the place, from a desert into a paradise.

A revolution broke out in the Philippines and even though Rizal was in no way connected with it, he was taken to Manila. All efforts were made by the authorities to secure evidence against him. His elder brother Paciano, was tortured into signing an accusation against Jose Rizal. But he, too, had the sacrificial qualities of a martyr and did not sign, and so he was hanged to death.

After a brief trial by the court martial, Jose Rizal was sentenced to be shot within twenty-four hours.

His mother and sister came to say farewell. Jose gave to his sister a little lamp, and talking to her in English, so that the guard could not understand, he told her, "There is something inside."

That something was a little ball of paper on which was written Jose Rizal's poem called the "Last Farewell", which is popular even today, as one of the best poems in Filipino literature.

Rizal was 36 years of age when he was led to the Begum Bayan field to be shot.

As eight soldiers fired together, with his last effort of will, Jose Rizal turned his body and fell face upward. Rizal was executed on the morning of 30 December, 1896. A wave of resentment spread over the Island that same day. Thousands of Filipinos poured in to join the revolution. The Spanish Friars fled to Madrid for their lives, leaving a thousand churches priestless.

Rizal had said:

I die, yet see, the skies glow overhead,

Announcing the day at last, beyond the night.

"The day" was finally announced eighteen months later when battle-ships from the United States silently stole into Manila Bay by night, and next morning sank the Spanish Fleet.

To this day, the Filipinos regard the spot of his execution as very sacred and revere it as a national shrine. The handsome young face of Rizal stands on a pedestal in every town and city of the Islands, urging the young Filipinos to stand up and sacrifice themselves in the name of patriotism.

Is not patriotism a great, heroic virtue? Is it not glorious to give up one's all for the sake of one's motherland and its people?

May we remember the great martyrs who laid their lives down for our country, even as we remember Rizal.

Fragrant be their memory!

Sayings of Jose Rizal

"While a people preserves its language; it preserves the marks of liberty."

"There can be no tyrants where there are no slaves."

"He who does not know how to look back at where he came from will never get to his destination."

"The youth is the hope of our future."

"Thou art my Mother, Mary, pure;
Thou'll be the fortress of my life;
Thou'll be my guide on this angry sea.
If ferociously vice pursues me,
If in my pains death harasses me,
Help me, and drive away my woes!"

"If truly a people dearly love
The tongue to them by Heaven sent,
They'll surely yearn for liberty
Like a bird above in the firmament."

"Lift up your radiant brow,
This day, Youth of my native strand!
Your abounding talents show
Resplendently and grand,
Fair hope of my Motherland!"

Some Books by Jose Rizal

- *Noli me tangere*
- *El Filibusterismo*
- *The Reign of Greed*
- *The Social Cancer*
- *The Revolution*
- *An Eagle Flight: A Filipino Novel*
- *Rèvolution Aux Philippines*
- *Poemas de Jose Rizal*

Some Books on Jose Rizal

- *Freedom's Martyr: The Story of Jose Rizal, National Hero of the Phillipines* (Avisson Young Adult Series) – by Suzanne Middendorf Arruda
- *Jose Rizal: Philippine Nationalist as Political Scientist* – by Howard DeWitt
- *Jose Rizal: Life, works, and writings of a genius, writer, scientist, and national hero* – by Gregorio F Zaide
- *Lineage, Life And Labors Of Jose Rizal* – by Austin Craig
- *On Wings of Destiny: a Novel on the Life and Times of Jose Rizal* – by Victoria Lopez De Araneta
- *Jose Rizal, Asia's first apostle of nationalism* – by Gregorio F Zaide
- *Lolo Jose: An intimate portrait of Rizal* – by Bantug, Asuncion Lopez
- *Rizal: Life, Works and Writings* – by Capino, Diosdado C., Gonzales, Ma. Minerva A. and Pineda

Shabri

Shabri was a simple tribal woman, whose outstanding characteristic was her deep and ardent devotion to the Lord. Accepted as a disciple by a renowned Guru, she was instructed to wait in his *ashrama* even after he passed away – for the Guru, in his wisdom, realised that she was one of the chosen ones, who would have a *darshana* of her *Ishtadevta* in her own lifetime. And so it came to pass. Sri Rama visited her, as promised, in her old age. And Shabri passed into the hearts of millions, passed into history as the devout woman who offered half-eaten fruits to the Lord!

Shabri

The story of Shabri is one of the most moving stories in our *puranas*.

Shabri was the daughter of the head of a forest-tribe. It was the eve of her wedding. Friends and relatives had gathered to join in the wedding festivities. With some of them she moved out for a short walk. On the way, she found a number of goats, lambs and fowls trapped in an enclosure. On their faces was the agony of approaching death. "What are they here for?" she asked. "To provide food for your wedding-feast!" they answered.

The words struck her with the force of a thunderbolt. The colour of her countenance changed. She returned home. She spoke to no one. She did not even have her dinner. She retired to a quiet corner. Within her heart were a hundred questions, all at once clamouring for answers. Is marriage worthwhile, if it involved the slaughter of so many innocent creatures of God, she asked herself. What happiness could she expect out of her married life which, before it began, was steeped in such cruelty? What is the purpose of life? What are the duties of man towards his younger brothers – birds and animals – in the one Family of creation?...

Shabri was sleepless through the night. Restless, she tossed and turned in her bed, until she firmly made a resolve. "Let the marriage scheduled to take place tomorrow," she said to herself, "be cancelled. I can have no part in such an unholy transaction!"

In the dark of the night, when all were asleep, Shabri got up. She did pranams to her father and mother and mentally sought their blessings. With one last, longing look, she surveyed her dearly-loved home, then swiftly moved out into the dark night.

Shabri was fearless. "The Great Heavenly Father who is at once my Father and the Father of all creatures who breathe the breath of life – will not forsake me!" she said to herself. True it is that He forsaketh none who, for His sake, forsakes the entire world. Shabri lived in the faith that He would take care of her, even as a mother would take care of her child. In her heart was child-like faith in God. And so she moved on from place to place, without fear, without anxiety.

Shabri met a *Rishi*, a sage who had communed with the mystery that is God. Shabri became his disciple and stayed with him for several years. She served him as a devoted daughter would serve a loving father.

The *Rishi* was advanced in years. One day, calling Shabri, he said, "My dearly loved daughter! The Call hath come to me! Tomorrow I go!"

Shabri did not understand. "Where will you go, leaving me here all alone? Why don't you take me with yourself?" she asked, puzzled.

"I go on the path on which two cannot travel together!" was his quiet answer.

There were tears in Shabri's eyes, as she said in a voice choked with emotion, "Not so, Gurudeva! Don't leave me here behind! But take me with yourself to the Homeland beyond the pathways of planets and stars."

The *Rishi* said to her lovingly, "Nay, my child! You have still to live for many more days. And so great is your good fortune that the Gods in Heaven envy you. For you are destined to meet Him – the Eternal One, the Lord Himself – who hath appeared in human disguise for the sake of the upliftment of His devotees.

"My child! He of whom I speak has appeared in Ayodhya as the Lord of the Raghus, Sri Rama – whose Name, in an instant, destroys countless sins of countless lives. He will soon become a homeless wanderer, moving for fourteen years, from forest to forest, filling with joy the hearts of innumerable devotees, clearing this ancient land of *asuras*, the demons, the evil ones!"

"How shall I recognise Him, Master?" Shabri enquired anxiously. And the *Rishi* said, "The moment you see Him, you will know Him! His body is dark as a wreath of blue lotuses, his eyes are radiant as bottomless pools in which is reflected the starlit sky. He will appear to you clad in a hermit's garb with bow and arrow in His hand, and with a quiver hanging at His side."

Shabri was wonder struck by the words of the departing *Rishi*. And she asked, "Master! Where shall I stay after you are gone?"

"Make your dwelling-place by the Lake Pampa," said the *Rishi*. "There will Sri Rama come to you and bless you out of the abundance of His mercy."

In utter loneliness lived Shabri in her solitary hut: but she never felt that she was alone. The thought of Sri Rama was her constant companion. She thought of Sri Rama: she meditated on Him: she repeated His Name, again and again, within her heart.

In the dead of the night, she got up and, unseen by human eyes, she swept the pathways which led from the *ashramas* of the *Rishis* to the lake. The *Rishis* were surprised to find the pathway always swept clean.

Shabri gave the love of her heart to birds and animals, to trees and flowers. "I am nothing," she said to herself. "May I become a speck on the Beloved's Lotus Feet!"

The day arrived when the news spread, from village to village, and from hut to hut, that the Beloved, Sri Rama, had arrived. The *Rishis* vied with each other for the honour of hosting Sri Rama. Princes arrived and pitched white tents in the hope that Sri Rama would accept their hospitality. In this keen contest, who thought of poor Shabri?

Only One there was, who thought of her. He was Sri Rama, the Eternal Friend of all who seek His refuge. And with unfaltering footsteps, He proceeded straight to the cottage of this unknown, humble, low-born woman. The princes looked in awe: the *Rishis* were humbled in their pride.

In Shabri's eyes were unbidden tears. She fell down and clung to Sri Rama's holy feet: she washed them with the tears that flowed from her eyes. She spoke not a word. When the heart is full, its language is a deep gaze and a spontaneous tear.

Shabri was poor, she had little to offer to her distinguished guests. In her simplicity, she brought to them roots and fruits and flowers. But before offering them to Sri Rama, she tasted them first, lest they be bitter or sour.

Sri Rama accepted the tasted fruit and ate it. His eyes sparkled! And to Lakshmana who was apparently intrigued, He said, "Lakshmana, never did I taste anything so delicious in my life!"

The values of the Lord are so unique, so different from human values. Our values are determined by a materialistic law of supply and demand. Calculative and speculative, we live in a world of narrow-mindedness. The true value of a gift, Sri Rama taught, was not in the rupees and paisas it could fetch in the market, but in the love which was enshrined within it.

To Shabri Sri Rama said, "Dear art thou to Me, O Shabri! For in thy heart is love, is faith, is humility.

Your caste matters not. For, verily, all the castes are Mine! And all religions, all races, all countries belong to Me!"

Sri Rama spoke to Shabri of nine ways in which a man might grow in the life of *bhakti*, of faith and love:

The first is *sanga*, fellowship with holy men. Fire kindles fire. Contact with the holy ones kindles within the heart, the flame of love.

The second is listening in faith and devotion to incidents from the lives of God-men, *shravana*. Daily contact with a holy man is not open to all. Listening to the life story of a holy man and meditating on his life in silence is, also, in a sense, fellowship with him.

The third is selfless service of the Guru and the *Sangat* (the Brotherhood of kindred souls). This, too, awakens love in the heart of the seeker.

The fourth is singing the praises of the Lord.

The fifth is repeating *Rama Nama, Hari Nama* – the Name of Rama, the Name of Hari, the Name of God. This repetition must not be a mechanical act.

The sixth is detachment which is rooted in self-control. Attachment leads to restlessness which is the cause of man's misery and anguish. Give up all attachment – to your work, your business, your friends, your family, your institution, your community, your nation, if you would grow in the love of God! And, detachment dawns on man when he realises that all desire is madness. It keeps him chained to the wheel of birth and death.

The seventh is to behold the One Lord everywhere. In every atom is He! In every leaf and flower, in every ray of light, in every drop of water, in every saint and sinner, and even in every bird and animal and tiny insect is He!

The eighth is to rejoice in God's Will and never to find fault with anyone.

The ninth is to live a life of utter simplicity, a life of child-like trust in God, our Divine Mother. She provides where She guides! What room then, is there for anxiety, for fear or depression?

Of those nine steps Sri Rama spoke to Shabri. There were tears in the eyes of Shabri. She was totally absorbed and lost in the Presence of the Beloved.

As Shabri listened, she became "unconscious". Her eyes no longer rained tears. Her voice was stilled. No more separation! Shabri had merged with the Beloved!

The true joy of life is at the Lotus Feet of the Beloved. And He wants of us no big things. The Lord wants little offerings of loving hearts. He who hath a loving heart himself becomes a little one. He eschews ambition, he renounces power, he gives up selfishness and greed. He becomes a servant of the poor and lowly, beholding in them images of God. And God enters the home of his heart and he is filled with joy supreme.

Some Books on Shabri

- Ramayana at a Glance – *By Sadguru Sant Keshavadas, Valmiki*
- *Folk Ballet of India* – by Rajendra Jain

Swami Leela Shah

Swami Leela Shah was an embodiment of simplicity and sincerity, selfless idealism and rigorous self-discipline. A magnetic spiritual leader, he turned his back on power, influence, wealth and prosperity to devote himself to a life fragrant with simplicity, purity and prayer. A staunch advocate of *yoga* and naturopathy, he made it his life's mission to spread the message of physical and spiritual health through simple living and high thinking.

Swami Leela Shah

Swami Leela Shah was one of the many Saints who have taken birth in the sacred land of Sind. He was born in the month of March in a small village. If I were asked to describe him in a few words, I would say: He was an embodiment of simplicity, service and sacrifice!

What is sacrifice? Sacrifice does not consist merely in giving up your home and family, smearing holy ash on your body, or wearing saffron robes. Sacrifice means giving up desires: it means conquering desire. It was Sri Ramakrishna Paramahansa who said, "A true saint, a real *Sadhu*, must keep away from two things — *kamini* (lust) and *kanchan* (gold)." Such a person beholds an image of his mother in every woman. He does not hanker after gold and worldly possessions!

Leela Shah's father was Shri Topandas and his mother was Hemibai. When Swami Leela Shah was still a child, both his parents passed away: he was brought up by his uncle. As a child, he did not show much interest in acquiring knowledge through books. He was fond of listening to *Bhagavat Kathas* and participating in *kirtans*. His heart would always move out to the poor and needy.

His uncle had a grocery store: Leela Shah had to look after it in the absence of his uncle. And at times he was asked to go and make purchases for the store. On the way if, perchance, he heard the cry of a poor beggar, he would give away something from the purchases he had made.

When Leela Shah was young, he came under the influence of a saint of God – Sant Keshavram. When Leela Shah was still a child, he had contracted jaundice. His family consulted doctors – but to no avail. Finally, they heard of Sant Keshavram. They took the child to him. The holy man checked the child's pulse and looked into his eyes. Sant Keshavram told the family, that Leela Shah would soon recover and get well, but the child would not be with them for long, for he belonged to Keshavram. The holy man's words came true. When Leela Shah was sixteen years of age, he became a disciple of Sant Keshavram. He chose to live the life of a *brahmachari*, a celibate. He was constantly pressurised by his relatives to get married, but he refused to do so. He had a deep longing to realise God and dedicate his life at His Lotus Feet, in the service of those that suffer and are in pain. Leela Shah lived a life of self-discipline and lost himself in the service of his Guru.

Leela Shah was greatly influenced by the teachings of Mahatma Gandhi and Shri Madan Mohan Malaviyaji, and sought to bear witness to their teaching in deeds of daily living. He was a man of spiritual magnetism and drew many to him in the service of God and His suffering children. If he had so wished, he could have accumulated a lot of wealth and attained a position of power and influence; but he had no such desire. When he passed away, he owned practically nothing!

There are some who give up wealth and are free from lust: yet in their hearts is the desire for name and fame. They hanker after praise and adulation. Leela Shah had a lot of followers but, like Sadhu Vaswani, he thought of himself as nothing. "We are but servants of God," he would say.

Leela Shah was the very picture of simplicity. He would wear a *khadi kurta* (long cotton shirt). He kept only two *kurtas* – one which was on his body and the other which he washed with his own hands.

He had an *ashrama* at Nainital. The *ashrama* comprised of two huts – one of which was for himself and the other for guests. He slept on the floor, and often walked barefoot. His hut had no door, only an entrance, which was so low, that one had to bend to enter it. This reminded the people who visited him, that to enter the kingdom of God, we must first become humble.

Let me tell you a little about his daily routine, so that you may know of his utter simplicity! He would get up at 4 a.m., brush his teeth with a *neem* twig, have a bath and then walk on the hills, where he would spend some time in silence and meditation. He would get back by nine or ten in the morning, and then have a vigourous massage with oil. He believed in physical fitness, for he respected the body as a shrine of the spirit.

After giving the body a massage, he would sit for half an hour, then take a bath and have lunch followed by a nap.

Even at the age of ninety five, he could walk briskly. He always did his own work. In preparing his food, he used pure ghee (clarified butter), for he believed it gave health and strength to the body.

When he had visitors, he would discuss with them the teaching of the *shastras* (scriptures). He would attend to his mail a number of people wrote to him for advice and guidance. He would go for a walk in the evening, and return at 8 p.m. This would be followed by *satsang*, after which he had his dinner and then he would go off to sleep.

After the "partition", Leela Shah migrated to India. He travelled from town to town, meeting people, comforting them and showing to them the way to be truly happy and healthy. He was a staunch advocate of *yoga* and naturopathy. He was a crusadar against the dowry system. He was a saviour of birds and animals–and a strong believer in vegetarianism. He established a number of *gaushalas*.

He urged that in order to be happy you must lead a simple life. "Living a life of pleasure will not give you the happiness you seek," he said.

He taught through precept and example that life has been gifted to us for two reasons. The first is to know ourselves: we identify ourselves with the body. But, we need to understand who we are, where we come from and what is the true purpose of our life on earth.

The second is *"paropkar"*, to help and serve others. For it is man's sacred duty to take care of the poor and needy, and also of birds and animals who are, as Sadhu Vaswani said, our younger brothers and sisters in the One Family of Creation.

Once Leela Shah visited the office of an engineer in the Public Works Department. The official was supervising the construction of a dam at that time. Leela Shah saw the water rising up against the wall of the dam, and the fish that were surging up to the surface were being caught by the crows, who swallowed them up in an instant. Leela Shah suggested to the engineer that a net might be spread out on the surface of the waters, to protect the fish. The engineer suggested, "These fish are food for the crows. How can I deprive the crows of their daily food?" Leela Shah replied, "It is our duty to protect as many lives as we can. God has His own way of providing for every creature!"

On November 4, 1973, at Palanpur, Swami Leela Shah dropped his physical body. His body was brought to Adipur (Gujarat), where his *Samadhi* was erected. Today, it is revered as a place of pilgrimage by his devotees.

Homage to him!

Sadna Kasai

Sadna Kasai was a butcher with a compassionate soul – a humble man whose devout yearning for God enabled him to attain a vision of the Divine. Sadna's tears were dearer to the Lord than the prayers and rituals performed by hermits and men of learning. Undeterred by misfortune, undaunted by the pain and suffering inflicted on him without cause, Sadna walked all the way to Puri to have the *darshan* of his Beloved, Sri Krishna. And the Lord granted him the divine bliss that many seek, and very few find.

Sadna Kasai

Sadhu Vaswani often used to refer to Sind, which is now a part of Pakistan, as a land of saints and sages, *darveshes* and *fakirs*. They were men and women of illumination. One such was Sadna.

Rare and inspiring was Sadna's life. He was a butcher by profession. From childhood, he had deep love for the Name Divine. Whenever he found even a little spare time, he would chant the Name of God; he would sing the glories of God!

Though he was a butcher by profession, he had a compassionate and loving heart. At times he would be so filled with compassion and love, that he would tremble at the very thought of killing birds and animals. This put him in a perennial dilemma, for on the one hand, he sold the flesh of birds and animals for his livelihood, and on the other, his heart wept with compassion for the creatures killed and eaten up. What was he to do? It was the only source of his livelihood. He had a family to take care of! Often he would get very dejected and disheartened. True, he would never slaughter the animals himself, but he did sell the flesh of creatures at his shop.

Whenever he had time to spare, he would call out with deep longing to Sri Krishna. He would chant the Holy Name of Sri Krishna. At times, he would be so engrossed in the Name of God, that he would even forget to eat or drink.

The longing for God kept increasing in Sadna's heart. Day by day, his yearning grew for a vision of God. He could not live, even for a moment, away from God.

One day, someone gave him a stone statuette or what is called *saligram*. He wondered what it was and what he could do with it. He had no idea of statues. He did not realise that it was an image of the Lord Sri Krishna whom, he loved with no ordinary love. He decided to use it as a measure of weight to weigh the flesh he sold. It was his habit to repeat the Name of Krishna constantly, with love and longing which, at times, brought unbidden tears to his eyes.

A hermit happened to pass by Sadna's shop, one day, and his eyes fell on the little statuette of Lord Krishna. He felt unhappy to find the way in which the sacred statuette was being used by the butcher. And he said to Sadna, "Will you kindly give me this weight measure?" Sadna gladly gave it away to the hermit. On receiving the statuette from Sadna, the hermit washed it and worshipped it with flowers.

How true it is that God is not happy with ritual worship! God is hungry for the love of the devotee's heart. God wants unsullied love, offered with deep devotion. The hermit would offer flowers and pray to Sri Krishna's statuette every single day. But Lord Krishna missed the love and longing, the deep yearning and devotion of Sadna. Lord Krishna appeared to the hermit, in a dream, and said to him, "Why have you separated Me from My dear, devoted disciple, Sadna? Whenever Sadna placed Me on his weighing scale, his touch filled with immense love and devotion, nourished Me. I enjoyed listening to Sadna's conversations! When he sang My Name, I danced in the Brindaban of his heart! O dear hermit, the tears of longing which drop from Sadna's eyes are more dear to Me than the rituals you follow and the bath you give Me everyday. The deep yearning with which he calls Me is more precious to Me than the chanting of your *mantras*. Therefore, dear hermit, please take Me back to Sadna's house."

In the morning, when he awoke, the hermit remembered the dream and rushed to Sadna's house and returned the statuette to him, saying, "You are the most fortunate amongst men, for you have immense love and longing in your heart for the Lord. And, do you know, you are the chosen one, for the Lord Himself loves you dearly!"

In a flash Sadna now realised that the weight-measure, which he had been using, was actually a little statue of the Lord Sri Krishna! He was deeply saddened, that he had failed to recognise the statuette for what it was; he repented greatly. He begged for forgiveness from Sri Krishna. How true it is that even if a man, in his ignorance or *avidya*, is disrespectful and derogatory towards God, yet God draws him closer to Himself! God never forsakes him.

Sadna shed tears. Every nerve of his body was saturated with the Name of Sri Krishna. How could he have offered disrespect to the statuette of the Lord?

Sadna no longer sold the flesh of animals. He closed his shop, and with the statuette of Sri Krishna in his hand, proceeded to Jagannath Puri. As he crossed village after village, he sang the glories of Sri Krishna. He kept walking till sunset. When he was hungry and tired, he would beg for food from the villagers. Thus he proceeded on his pilgrimage.

One night, he halted at a village, and, as usual, received food and shelter. However, his handsome, graceful and beautiful form attracted a lustful woman, the wife of a villager. The woman approached him and tried to tempt him. "You are dearer to me than my own breath," she said. "We both should get intimate with each other."

Sadna heard those words and was greatly disturbed. He ignored the woman and continued chanting the Name of Sri Krishna. "Mother," he said to the woman, "you too, must sing the Name of God with me! It will purify you."

The woman was surprised at his attitude. But she was not the one to give up easily. "Maybe, he is afraid of my husband," she thought to herself. In the dark of the night, she picked up a sword and chopped off her husband's head. She came to Sadna and said, "The deed has been accomplished. I have got rid of my husband. He was the one obstacle between the two of us, was he not? Let us live together and enjoy life!"

Sadna was stunned. "O you wicked woman," he screamed. "This is not love, this is lust, it is mere gratification of the senses. Return to your home and repent for your sins and chant the Name of the Lord:

> Hare Krishna! Hare Krishna! Krishna Krishna, Hare Hare!
> Hare Rama! Hare Rama! Rama Rama, Hare Hare!"

When the woman found that she could not entice Sadna, she decided to teach him a lesson. She stood on the threshold of her house and wailed bitterly. "Sadna has murdered my husband! To gratify his lust, he killed my husband! What shall I do now?"

The villagers, on hearing her cries, gathered at her house. Sadna listened to the woman's words, but he continued to chant, "Krishna, Krishna, Krishna!" With deep yearning in his heart, he kept on repeating, "Krishna! Krishna! Krishna!" The villagers, of course, were carried away by the woman's false accusations. Without verifying the facts, they caught Sadna and beat him up and would not let him alone till he confessed to the murder. Sadna however, was lost in chanting the Name of God. He was unaffected.

The villagers then dragged Sadna to a court of law and narrated the fabricated story to the judge. Sadna did not protest. His faith in Sri Krishna was firm. He heard everything silently. He watched the *leela* of the Lord unfolding. All he said was, "I am not guilty, but how do I prove my innocence?"

The judge saw his condition and was in a fix. Instead of hanging him, he ordered that both Sadna's hands be cut off.

The sentence was carried out: Sadna's hands were chopped off. Though he was in tremendous pain, he bore it all, patiently, uncomplainingly. There was a smile of compassion on his lips, as he continued to recite the Holy Name. He thought to himself, "Surely this is the fruit of my *karmas*: for years together I worked as a butcher. I should have been hanged, but Krishna, in His mercy, has given me a light punishment. Blessed be His Name! Krishna! Krishna! Krishna!" With a prayer in his heart for the woman, Sadna proceeded on his journey to Jagannath Puri.

Arriving there, he found the Chief Priest of the Temple waiting for him. Sri Krishna had appeared in a dream to the Chief Priest and had said to him, "My beloved devotee – Sadna by name – is coming to the Temple. Go and greet him and bring him to the temple with all the honours, in a chariot."

The Chief Priest asked, "Lord, how shall I know him?"

And Sri Krishna answered, "You will know him when you see him, for his hands have been chopped off!"

Sadna was brought to the Temple, in a chariot, with all honours. On his lips were the words: "Krishna, Krishna, Krishna!" As soon as Sadna entered the Jagannath Temple, we are told, a miracle happened. His hands were restored to him! He and all who beheld the miracle, were wonderstruck. Sadna shed tears of joy and glorified the Lord.

Sadna spent his time in singing the Name of God and helping the people who were around him. He beheld the Image of his Beloved Krishna in everyone. Again and again, he cried: "Wherever I turn, I see Thee and Thee alone! I see Thee in everything – in star and in stone!"

He accepted everything that happened to him. He never questioned the wisdom of God. "There is a meaning of mercy in all that happens," he urged.

One night, he had a meaningful dream. Sri Krishna appeared in the dream and said to him, "In your earlier birth you were born as a Brahmin in Kashi. One day, a cow was about to be slaughtered by a butcher. She managed to escape and the butcher ran after her, trying to catch her. You happened to pass that way and the butcher called out to you for help. You helped him in capturing the cow, with both your hands. The cow was subsequently slaughtered. The wicked woman, whose false accusation caused your hands to be cut off, was that cow in her previous birth, and her husband was the butcher. The woman killed her husband. And since you assisted the butcher in catching the cow, your hands were cut off. Whatever happens to man is his own *karma* coming back to him."

Sadna related this dream to his friends and fellow-devotees and said, "We must never complain about what is happening to us. In every incident and accident of life there is a meaning of God's mercy. Therefore, let this be the rule of our life: "Stop complaining: Start thanking!"

Let us reflect on these wise words: 'Stop complaining! Start thanking.' Let us put this valuable precept into practise: Let us stop complaining; let us start thanking the Lord!

Zarathustra

Zarathustra was a Persian Prophet and poet, who founded the unique, peace-loving religion now known by the name of Zoroastrianism. A great sage and spiritual leader, he faced opposition and threats from his own people, before he gained acceptance. He became a martyr – but his teachings continue to live on in East and West.

Zarathustra

Zoroaster, also known as Zarathustra, is saluted as a Messenger of God by many. According to one report, he was born approximately one thousand years before Christ, in what was then known as Persia.

As we all know, every child is born into this world with a cry, a wail. Of Zarathustra, it is said that the new-born babe greeted this world with a loud burst of laughter!

All nature seemed to rejoice at his coming: the rivers and the running brooks, the woods and the hills, the lilies of the field and the lotuses in the lake, seemed to sing in joy.

The baby was beautiful to behold. The light of purity shone in his eyes; a benevolent smile played upon his lips. They named him Zarathustra – which means 'Lover of camels'. He would live up to that name, by feeding other people's cattle from his father's barn.

As he grew into boyhood, it was obvious that he was quite different from other children. Many were the wonderful deeds he did, even at that age. Often, he would give away his food to a passing beggar, while he himself stayed hungry. He would distribute all his playthings amongst his friends, keeping nothing for himself.

At the age of seven, Zarathustra was sent to study under a teacher well-renowned for his knowledge and wisdom. For the next eight years, Zarathustra sat at the feet of his Master, to receive the knowledge of the Sun, Moon, Stars and Celestial bodies in their orbits, the cycle of the seasons, the light, the wind and the rain, of men, birds and animals – and the great Creator of the Universe.

As he grew in years, he grew also in the quality of compassion. His heart flowed in a stream of sympathy to all living creatures. It is said, that he once bought bread to feed a dying dog, and offered the creature some comfort in its last hours.

When he was just fifteen years old, he moved away from the world of men, to meditate in the seclusion of the forest, in a cave on the Mount Sabalon. He meditated for long on the Mystery of Life, and the Wonder that is the World. He communed with Ahura Mazda – the Spirit of Life and Light and Love. He beheld Him face to face, and spoke to Him, even as a son would speak to his father.

From time to time, he descended from the mountain-heights to the plains below. He mingled with men. He shared his food with the hungry; he gave away his clothes to the needy; he served the aged and the infirm. He healed the sick. He lightened the loads of the burden-bearing camels and horses. He comforted the forsaken and forlorn with his loving words: he offered them hope and cheer on their lonely way, blessing them and healing their broken hearts.

For fifteen years, he continued to live this life – a life of meditation and communion with the Highest, and of service and compassion to the least of the little ones. When he was thirty years of age, he came back to live among his people. His face shone as molten gold; in his eyes was the light of wisdom; he had been illumined by a Divine Revelation, initiated by a series of seven blessed visions!

For the next ten years, he moved through the towns and the villages of his native land, proclaiming the Truth that had been revealed to him. Not once did he get an eager, receptive audience, willing to listen to him. The people were just not ready to receive from the Prophet the revelation meant for them and the rest of mankind. He was greeted with jeers and howls wherever he went; they even pelted stones at him, inflicting wounds on his pure, sacred body. He bore in gentle and loving patience the pain and the scorn heaped upon him. On his lips was the smile of mercy and in his heart was the prayer: "O Ahura Mazda! Have mercy on them and lead them out of the darkness of the Evil One, into the Light of Thy Truth!"

At last, he found someone who would stand by him and accept the truth of his teachings. His cousin, Metyoma, came up to him, saying, "Zarathustra! I believe in thee and thy mission! Permit me to follow thee!"

Together, they moved, from place to place, two lone pilgrims of Ahura Mazda. Together they preached, together they served and suffered, knowing fully well that triumph would always belong to Truth.

And indeed, Truth triumphed, ultimately! The day arrived when Zarathustra was hailed as a Prophet by the very people by whom he had been persecuted earlier.

In the course of his wanderings, Zarathustra came one day to Balkh, the capital of ancient Iran, where King Vishtaspa held his court. There was something about the Prophet, some glow in his looks, some magic in his words, that cast a spell on the King. Clad in pure white, flowing garments, bearing in one of his hands a staff of cypress wood, and in the other, the sacred fire, Zarathustra's appearance worked a transformation on the King. This conqueror of many lands and many armies was conquered by the Truth of the Prophet. He was happy to surrender himself to the Messenger of God, whose only weapons were love and righteousness.

The Truth of his faith was now triumphant. Wherever he went, crowds of people followed him – no longer to pelt him with stones, but to revere him and touch the hem of his garment in love and devotion. For this Prophet was also a healer of souls – he reclaimed lost souls with the Holy Word of God. In his sacred text, the *Vendidad*, Zarathustra tells us, "There are healers of different types; there are those who heal with the knife: and there are those who heal with herbs. But the best is even he who heals with the Holy Word."

Such was his power, that Zarathustra cured men afflicted with diverse deadly diseases. He gave sight to the blind. It is said that he even brought the dead to life.

The influence of Zoroaster's teachings spread as far as Greece and Rome. Socrates was said to have a Zoroastrian instructor named Gobyras. It was said that Plato, too, wished to visit Persia to study with Zoroastrian teachers, but could not undertake the proposed journey due to the outbreak of a local war.

What were Zarathustra's teachings? He looked around him and saw all creation burdened by anxiety, groaning in pain and misery. He felt the agony and anguish of human hearts. He perceived the unshed tears in the eyes of birds and animals. He called upon every man to enlist himself in the Army of God.

"Be ye warriors of Light!" he said to all who heard him.

"What may we do to belong to the Army of God?" people asked him.

"Walk the way of righteousness!" was his simple answer.

"How may we walk the way of righteousness?" they persisted.

Clear and simple, direct and profound was his reply: "Build your life in good thoughts, good words, good deeds!"

The root cause of man's suffering, he taught, was ignorance – what the Gita calls *avidya*. "It is ignorance," said Zarathustra, "which drags many men to their ruination. For men, in their ignorance, do not realise that when they injure another, they cause harm to themselves. All humanity is one family and I can be happy only when my brothers and sisters are happy."

"Banish ignorance with the light of wisdom," he urged, again and again.

"What are the primary duties of man?" he was asked.

"These three," he replied, "First, to convert an enemy into a friend; second, to teach righteousness to the wicked; and third, to spread the light of wisdom, where ignorance abounds – for wisdom is richer than all the wealth of the world."

Zarathustra moved, from place to place, with his message of righteous living. His message brought about a revolution in the hearts and minds of his people. It called them away from a life of sordid selfishness to a larger, higher, more beautiful life of loving fellowship and service of the needy. It infused in their hearts a new faith in God and goodness.

For forty-seven years Zarathustra continued to pass on his message to rich and poor, princes and peasants. Then came the day, which cometh in the life of all men, wherever they may be – the Day of Farewell from this earthly pilgrimage.

It is believed by some of the faithful that the Prophet was carried away by a stroke of lightning; yet others believe that he was assassinated while conducting worship in his Temple.

I do not know how it was – I only know that such a One as Zarathustra can never die! The seasons may tire and the years may grow old. But the life and teachings of this great Messenger of God will continue to spread their radiance, far and wide!

Sayings of Zarathustra

"Devotion, like fire, goeth upward."

* * * * *

"He who sows the ground with care and diligence acquires a greater stock of religious merit than he could gain by the repetition of ten thousand prayers."

* * * * *

"When you doubt, abstain."

* * * * *

"Doing good to others is not a duty, it is a joy, for it increases our own health and happiness."

* * * * *

"Turn yourself not away from three best things: Good Thought, Good Word, and Good Deed."

* * * * *

"Taking the first footstep with a good thought the second with a good word and the third with a good deed I entered Paradise."

* * * * *

Ability in a man is knowledge which emanates from divine light.

* * * * *

All flows out from the Deity, and all must be absorbed in Him again.

* * * * *

Do not hold grain waiting for higher prices when people are hungry.

Some Books by Zarathustra

- *The Gathas of Zarathustra : Hymns in Praise of Wisdom* – Translated by Piloo Nanvutty
- *The Gathas of Zarathustra (English)* – Translated by Stanley Insler
- *The Last Four Gathas of Zarathustra and Legends* – by Albert Pike
- *Gathas of Zarathustra: Text* – by Yasna Avesta

Some Books on Zarathustra

- *In Search of Zarathustra: Across Iran and Central Asia to Find the World's First Prophet* – by Paul Kriwaczek
- *"Thus Spake Zarathustra"* – by Friedrich Nietzsche
- *The Zend Avesta of Zarathustra*
- *Zoroastrian Tradition: An Introduction to the Ancient Wisdom of Zarathustra* – by Farhang Mehr
- *Zarathustra's Secret* – by Joachim Kohler